T0294813

A Practical Guide
to Fundraising
for Small Museums

A Practical Guide to Fundraising for Small Museums

Maximizing the Marketing-Development Connection

Sheldon Wolf

ROWMAN & LITTLEFIELD
Lanham • Boulder • New York • London

Rowman & Littlefield Publishers, Inc.
A wholly owned subsidiary of The Rowman & Littlefield Publishing Group, Inc.
4501 Forbes Boulevard, Suite 200
Lanham, Maryland 20706

British Library Cataloguing in Publication Information Available

Library of Congress Cataloging-in-Publication Data

ISBN: 978-1-5381-0325-8 (cloth : alk. paper)
ISBN: 978-1-5381-0326-5 (pbk. : alk. paper)
ISBN: 978-1-5381-0327-2 (electronic)

∞™ The paper used in this publication meets the minimum requirements of American National Standard for Information Sciences—Permanence of Paper for Printed Library Materials, ANSI/NISO Z39.48-1992.

Printed in the United States of America

CONTENTS

LIST OF FIGURES

LIST OF TABLES

PREFACE

"Collections have no needs. People do. Collections don't know if they are being appreciated. Collections don't know if they are being cared for properly. People know. We are not here for the collections; we are here for people."

This is how I began a presentation in 1992, my first, to what was then the American Association of Museums (now the American Alliance of Museums) in Baltimore. I had been asked to talk about how I was achieving so much success during a recession at my relatively small museum complex in Springfield, Massachusetts. The name I had given the program was "Seizing the Day: An Optimist's Approach to Development in a Pessimist's World." I began with the thoughts noted above. "Collections have no needs. People do." After just those few sentences, several people rose from their seats and left the room, apparently in disgust. For curators at that time, what I was suggesting was sacrilege. But as I continued to talk about an approach to development that was focused on donors rather than on the organizations for which we work (or the objects within), something remarkable happened. I heard someone go to the back of the small program room and call into the hallway, "Hey, you have to hear this guy." By the end of the program, seventy-five minutes long, several hundred people were crowded into a space where I had anticipated perhaps fifty. I don't think that what I was presenting was so revolutionary. Like a photographer, all I was doing was shifting the focus.

A few years later, an outstanding professional growth opportunity occurred for me when my daughter was completing her college applications.

Mixed in with the standard lists of activities and recommendations was an unusual question from a prominent university. The applicants were asked to read a lengthy article from *Atlantic Monthly* in which a panel of intellectuals discussed the impact of technology on various aspects of contemporary life. In her essay, my daughter noted that, despite the range of electronic means available for staging this lengthy academic dialogue, the four panelists had chosen to meet in person in a restaurant in Manhattan where, over a fine lunch and some wine, they debated the pros and cons of advancing technology. The lunch meeting was transcribed as the basis for the article, a bit like the film *My Dinner with André*. My daughter's essay focused on the panelists' choice of direct and personal contact rather than use of available technology. What an odd choice for four techno-wizards!

If my own priorities are defined by how I've spent my time as a development professional, then I've bought into the supremacy of technology. I've learned new web search techniques, mastered various formats for storing and retrieving data, and I can produce a snazzy report. But the sad reality is that I've devoted much less time than I should have learning more about interpersonal techniques or nonverbal communication. What I know about human behavior comes from reading books (novels in particular), a bit of training many years ago as a group counselor, and a great deal of observation. With so much development work focused on one-to-one interaction, shouldn't person-to-person skills be just as important to my profession as a workshop in the latest software upgrade? Where do we see such training offered? Certainly not at professional conferences.

I don't think I'm alone, and this frightens me. As a profession, have we become experts in the electronic tools of our craft even while we have abandoned learning about what makes people tick? Shouldn't we spend at least as much time learning how to keep eye contact as we do learning how to craft direct mail?

My daughter was accepted by the big university, but she chose a much more adventurous course of study at another fine institution. Her school of choice had nowhere near as many computers as some other major universities, but all of the classes were taught by professors, in person.

"I'm there to learn about people from people, Dad," my daughter said.

Sometimes our kids just get it.

That AAM talk was the first of many programs I have presented for various national and regional museum organizations, as well as for other groups concerned with nonprofit management. I did not know at the time that one program could begin a path to a book.

In *A Practical Guide to Fundraising for Small Museums: Maximizing the Marketing-Development Connection*, I seek first to bridge the gap found in too many museums between various functions. Too often, decisions that impact marketing, membership, or development are made in some other area, such as curatorial, without any participatory conversation. I hope to empower the staff and encourage the interdepartmental dialogue that is essential for success. Second, I seek to provide some new ways to think about development as part of a relationship-building team that is intertwined with everyone else who works for or with the museum. Many books on museum development begin with the idea of a donor pyramid; people become members, and then some of them become donors, and then a few of them become major donors, and so forth until we talk about a small group of planned gift donors. If we are truly concerned about relationships, we must look at the very beginnings of the public getting to know us. Otherwise, it is like wondering about relationships but starting with the third date. How do visitor prospects in our market know us? How do they decide to visit? What motivates them to come to a museum a second time or a third? *A Practical Guide to Fundraising for Small Museums* moves the process back to the basic questions of what we are about and what our public is all about. We begin with people. Then we can think about giving.

If we look at our institutional mission statements, they are likely to include a phrase such as "to serve the people of . . ." or "for the people of . . ." some region. We create museums in order to serve people.

A Practical Guide to Fundraising for Small Museums is largely about people. I'm not going to talk about software. You will find some charts and graphics, and, of course, metrics are important, but ultimately development is about understanding people. We will examine the progression of public involvement from how the marketplace first knows about the museum to transactional decisions to attend and then to join. Then *A Practical Guide to Fundraising for Small Museums* explores giving that is more relational, more tied to support for the museum's mission: annual fund and major gifts. We will look at other ways to build on relationships to raise money through tributes, grants, and corporate giving. Success in all of these areas creates the necessary foundation for planned gifts and a capital campaign. Finally, I provide some thoughts on surviving in the stressful but rewarding world of raising money.

The more we know about a) people in general and b) the people in our particular service area, the more effective we will be in our development work. The buildings themselves, or the organizational structures we have established, the software we use, and, yes, the collections, are the means we have for serving the needs of people.

ACKNOWLEDGMENTS

Special thanks to Joseph Carvalho III, Martin Cohen, The Cornerstone Studio (East Hills, New York), Donna Freyman and Richard Stup, Nancy Gaddy, Linda and Allen Greenbaum, Charles Harmon, Dana Hines, Roanne Katcher, Kathleen O'Brien, Diane Ward, Evelyn and Jeff Weller, and the entire clan of Wolf family members and friends for their encouragement, and especially to Betsy Wolf, for everything.

CHAPTER ONE

THE MARKETING-
DEVELOPMENT CONNECTION

You miss 100% of the shots you don't take.

—Wayne Gretzky

What Is a Small Museum?

What is a small museum? Is a small museum defined by budget? If so, a museum that has grown from no budget to a small budget faces a different set of issues from a museum that once had a much larger budget and squandered away its money. A small museum located in farm country on a dirt road is quite different from a small museum that strives for attention in a museum-rich major metropolitan area. A small museum that focuses on a national figure (let's say Abraham Lincoln) has a different set of issues from a similarly small museum that focuses on the history of East Anywhere, USA. Although both museums are physically small, the Lincoln museum has wider audience potential than the "East Anywhere" museum with its more limited regional mission. Recognizing that difference will lead to more realistic expectations and is critical to the success of each institution.

A Practical Guide to Fundraising for Small Museums: Maximizing the Marketing-Development Connection suggests a people-centered approach. Rather than a specific set of answers or guidelines, think of the ideas presented here as different ways to question your work. The answers to those questions, what is "right" for you and your museum, may be quite different from the answers for the museum across town or the museum across the country.

1

The path to success for you begins with learning your audience. Everything else follows.

The 4 Ps: Product, Price, Place, Promotion

The first victim was a twelve-year-old girl in suburban Chicago. To treat her sore throat and runny nose, her parents had given her an Extra-Strength Tylenol. By 7:00 the next morning, the girl was dead.

That same day, a postal worker in another Chicago-area town died. At first, it was thought he had suffered a heart attack. Then it was revealed that he too had taken Extra-Strength Tylenol. Then there was another victim, and then another. Soon, the entire country was in a panic. The Tylenol in question had been laced with a lethal dose of cyanide. Who else had taken Tylenol?

The year was 1982. I wonder what it was like during those scary days to be working in the marketing department for McNeil Laboratories, the makers of Tylenol. What words could possibly calm the American public? How would McNeil (and its parent company, Johnson & Johnson) ever regain the trust of American consumers?

Fast forward to now. Those of us who work in museums are unlikely to face decisions of life or death. Perhaps that is my first bit of advice to those who enter the noble profession of museum development. What we do is important to our communities, to our volunteers, to our colleagues, and to our own egos, but the choices we make about how to perform our jobs will not mean life or death. With that perspective, too often those involved with marketing and development are confronted with the dual demands of "bring more people" and "bring more money." The assumption (sometimes from the executive director, sometimes from the board) seems to be that if only we knew the secret concoction of magic advertising words, we could somehow unlock the vaults of endless wealth.

I don't know those magic words. No one does.

But I do know, just as the good folks at McNeil Laboratories knew in 1982, that good marketing (and therefore good development) begins with the product. No amount of fancy language would have assuaged the fears of those who had taken Tylenol. The first step was not a new ad campaign or a new brochure. The first step was to take the bad product off the shelves. By the end of the massive recall, more than thirty-one million bottles of Tylenol were removed from circulation. Free replacement bottles were offered to those who had Extra-Strength Tylenol at home. Fortunately, only a few tainted bottles were discovered. Only then could the rebuilding of the corporate brand begin.

Good development is a form of good marketing, and good marketing begins with the product.

What is the product?

That very first marketing decision likely began when the founders of your museum decided what type of museum they wanted. Would it be a children's museum? If so, some of the audience and funding issues you now face were cast right at the beginning. Children's museums attract an audience largely of young families with children. As the children get older, the parents' interest in the children's museum wanes, and ultimately most of these families move on to something else. Children's museums experience a good deal of "churn" in their memberships, with large percentages of members opting out each year, replaced by new younger families. Art museums tend to attract a much older audience. Even with efforts to create children's art corners and summer camps for kids, most of the attendees will be older, educated adults. Science museums, zoos, and aquaria fall somewhere in the middle. The subject matter appears to be more accessible (everyone knows how to identify a lion, a shark, or a gemstone, right?), so the leisure time decision-making parents think they will be less intimidated. Audiences hold on for a while. Then, beyond the prime years of family participation, many people understand how a science museum supports classroom instruction. Perhaps this works for history too. Art may be a little tougher; for example, "How does seeing this painting help my child get a job?" The point behind all of these assumptions is that the subject matter of your museum, probably based on your collections and something not likely to change, is your main product decision, leading to numerous consequences in audience and donor behavior.

Going to a museum is a choice similar to eating out. Think of all the factors that go into a decision to go to a restaurant. First, there is likely to be the question of the kind of food. ("Do I like that kind of food? Will I know what to order?") The kind of food is related to questions about the kind of museum. Some people will opt in or out based on just that one factor.

Then, if you haven't been there before:

- Will I see people like me there?

- What do I hear about it?

3

- What do the reviews say?

- What kind of promotion is involved (colors, images, language)?

- Is it convenient? Parking? Will I have to walk far?

- Is it expensive?

If you've been to the restaurant before:

- Was the food good?

- Was it a good value?

- How was the service? Timely? Friendly staff?

- Was it clean?

- Could I linger, or was I rushed?

Notice that although restaurants seem to be about food, the food selection is ultimately just one of the elements that influence the decision to go or not go. All of those elements of food, service, cleanliness, etc. are part of the product, part of the total offering. As Joseph Pine II and James H. Gilmore propose in their book *The Experience Economy*, restaurants are really theatrical performances with actors (waiters, hosts), set (décor), script (the menu, how the menu is presented by the waiter), props, etc. Even the customers (certainly the other customers one sees at other tables) are part of the show. One doesn't just buy food. One buys the whole *experience*.

"When designing your experience, you should consider the following questions:

- What can be done to improve the *esthetics* of the experience? The esthetics are what make your guests want to come in, sit down, and hang out. Think about what you can do to make the environment more inviting, interesting, or comfortable. You want to create an atmosphere in which your guests feel free 'to be.'

- Once there, what should your guests do? The *escapist* aspect of an experience draws your guests further, immersing them in activities. Focus on what you should encourage guests 'to do' if they are to become active participants in the experience.

- The *educational* aspect of the experience, like the escapist, is essentially active. Learning, as it is now largely understood, requires the full participation of the learner. What do you want your guests 'to learn' from the experience? What information or activities will help to engage them in the exploration of knowledge and skills?

- *Entertainment*, like esthetics is a passive aspect of the experience. When your guests are entertained, they're not really doing anything but responding to (enjoying, laughing at, etc.) the experience. . . . How can you make the experience more fun and enjoyable?" (Pine and Gilmore, 39–40)

What are the elements that make up the museum experience? (This list is adapted from ideas presented in Mokwa et al., *Marketing the Arts*, 23–25.) Here are some aspects of a museum visit as experienced by a visitor:

- Promotion: colors, images, language

- Parking or accessibility

- Facility: neighborhood (safety, access to transportation, other sites nearby); banners and signs; décor; cleanliness; imposing or homey; coatroom

- Welcome: staff (front desk, guards); maps or guides; wayfinding throughout the museum

- Audience: crowds or small audience; elite or "just folks"; sophisticated in their knowledge of the subject or novices

- Exhibitions: permanent and changing; the number and type; the quality; the subject matter; ease of understanding; interpretative tools such as labels, wall signage and handouts, as well as audio tours, collection apps, etc.

- Programs: when scheduled?; what length?; beginner or advanced; communication skills of the presenters

- Amenities: café; gift shop; places to sit

Any of these factors can influence the decision to return or not. How can anyone be expected to raise money for exhibitions that are subpar, for programs that do not engage the public, for poor standards of collection care, or for lack of concern for the visitor experience? In order for development efforts to excel, the product *must* be excellent.

Many definitions of marketing focus only on communicating a message that informs and educates targeted consumers. Messages about what?

Here are a few definitions that highlight a *complete* sequence of marketing activities:

> Marketing is the activity, set of institutions, and processes for creating, communicating, delivering, and exchanging offerings that have value for customers, clients, partners, and society at large.
>
> — American Marketing Association

> Marketing is not only much broader than selling; it is not a specialized activity at all. It encompasses the entire business. It is the whole business seen from the point of view of the final result, that is, from the customer's point of view. Concern and responsibility for marketing must therefore permeate all areas of the enterprise.
>
> — Peter Drucker

Even if yours is a museum with a staff of one with no designated budget for promotion, you are marketing. Your choice of activities, your building, your pricing structure, the people who are involved with you, and the words you choose to describe your work are sending messages to your public.

In the best marketing programs, those activities involve conscious choices and understanding about how those choices may impact your current and potential audiences. Why this exhibit rather than that? Why this entrance fee rather than another? Why these hours? Why these people on our staff, board, or volunteer committee? And on and on.

The online *Business Directory* says that marketing is "the management process through which goods and services move from concept to the customer. It includes the coordination of four elements called the 4 Ps of marketing:

1. identification, selection and development of a **product**,

2. determination of its **price**,

3. selection of a distribution channel to reach the customer's **place**, and

4. development and implementation of a **promotional** strategy."

As noted above, a museum's product includes everything it does for the public (exhibitions, programs), the kinds of information it provides, everything that is part of the visitor experience (public transportation, parking, walkways, signage, ticket buying procedures, rest rooms). The building is part of the product. The landscaping. The neighborhood. Is there a café? Coatroom? Gift shop?

Okay, I can hear the objections. "But we can't change our building." "But we've always been free." "But we don't have room for anything else." "We can't afford to do it better." "But . . ."

Change what you can change. If something cannot be changed, at least recognize and acknowledge to your staff and board how it ultimately impacts your development efforts.

Product comes first.

Then, how you price your museum experience says quite a bit about you. Most museums have several tiers of pricing: general admission, free admission for select groups (most often at least members), and various discount offerings (often through affiliation with other organizations such as the Automobile Association of America or a local arts marketing collaborative). Some museums, especially those that receive most of their funding from local government sources, provide free general admission for everyone. Above and beyond the cost of the entry ticket, most museums charge for additional programs and services, such as lectures, films, and concerts.

Surveys of your various audiences will help you understand how your price structure is perceived in your marketplace and how it influences the decision to visit or not to visit. Some audiences will understand the need to be free. Others might misinterpret "free" as "having no value." For example, imagine driving down a country road and coming across two signs. One sign says, "Antique Furniture for Sale." The second sign, just across the road, says, "Antique Furniture—Free." In this case, many people might assume that "free" equals "junk."

Alternatively, admission that is too high may equate to "not a good value" or "I cannot afford to go." While mounting a special exhibition in Smalltown, USA, may cost the same as mounting the same exhibition in Big

Tourist Town, the Smalltown museum market may not tolerate the same admission price structure as the large city museum.

Because reduced or free admission is often a benefit of membership (discussed in more detail shortly), how does your admission structure relate to your membership program? At higher-priced museums, zoos, and aquaria, heads of families are often seen at the ticket counter calculating the benefit: "If an adult ticket is X and a child ticket is Y, and if I come back twice, I'll be ahead of the game financially." The trick in this exchange is that the buyer must believe that a second visit is likely, that either there is so much to see that one visit will not provide enough time for the whole experience, or some new and desirable experience/exhibition is coming up later in the membership year. In short, the pricing structure reverts back to the product: Is it worth it?

In our digital age, the number of places where your museum presents its programs and services has become more complicated. For most museums, the hub of activity is the museum building. Is it in a heavily traveled part of downtown or is it set in a bucolic but isolated setting removed from potential visitors? Is the building in an area served by public transportation, or is it within walking distance of hotels and other tourist amenities? If visitors must drive, is there adequate parking nearby? How do parking fees impact the overall cost of the day? Is the museum a temple of culture reached by imposing steps and an august façade, or is it a contemporary design that discreetly hides the front door?

What is the clarity and arrangement of spaces inside? Is wayfinding intuitive, or will visitors feel lost? Are public programs held in the galleries (perhaps disturbing contemplative visitors), or are programs in a well-designed theater located in an out-of-the-way hallway?

What is the overall ambiance? Are there many other (or too many other) visitors in the museum? Some people will be intimidated by a museum that is too quiet.

Some programs and services, such as online collection catalogues and podcasts of lectures, are now virtual. Are such programs free or is there a fee? Or are they available only as a member benefit? If you do or do not offer such virtual learning opportunities, what is the message to computer-savvy audiences?

Promotion is the end of this process. Unfortunately, many "marketers," perhaps wanting to place a tangible imprint on the museum, start with a new logo design or a new brochure. Instead, start with the more fundamental questions: Who are you? What is your value to your consumers? How is your place helping or hindering your product offerings?

As much as possible, the answers to these questions must result from organization-wide discussion and deliberate decision making. Each answer will assist or diminish your ability to attract visitors. When you are clear on product, price, and place, you are ready to call in the writers and the designers.

Product. Price. Place. Promotion. For whom are you doing this work?

Know Your Customers

What do your customers (visitors) think about your product (the museum experience)? The best way to fund out how visitors perceive your museum is to ask. Asking may be accomplished in several ways:

- On-site surveys of many visitors
- Extended intercepts of a smaller number of visitors
- Focus groups
- Mystery "shoppers"

If we don't know what the visitors are thinking, we cannot know what to keep and what to change. But if we ask, we must be prepared to listen. The results may be difficult, and some of your staff colleagues may put up considerable resistance to adjustments. Sometimes we in development may find ourselves on a collision course with our curators. We and they often work on different cycles. They live with an exhibition for an extended time. The exhibition opens, and the curator must move on to the next project. But now marketing and development must live with the exhibition, perhaps for years. Be considerate. Be respectful. But be firm. If something is not working, it is to everyone's benefit to make a correction.

In *A Passion for Excellence* by Tom Peters and Nancy Austin, the first several chapters are focused on the customer experience. The authors present the following copy that is prominently displayed all around the facilities and on the website of the Freeport, Maine, retailer L.L. Bean:

What Is a Customer?
A Customer is the most important person ever in this office . . . in person or by mail.

A Customer is not dependent on us . . . we are dependent on him.

A Customer is not an interruption of our work . . . he is the purpose of it. We are not doing him a favor by serving him . . . he is doing us a favor by giving us the opportunity to do so.

A Customer is not someone to argue or match wits with. Nobody ever won an argument with a Customer.

A Customer is a person who brings us his wants. It is our job to handle them profitably to him and to ourselves. (Peters and Austin, 111–112)

Peters and Austin also highlight the practice of "Management by Walking the Floor" (Peters and Waterman, 289). This means that one of the best ways of understanding the visitor experience is by observing visitors in action. How do they enter the museum? Are they clear about what to do next? How do they view an exhibition? Do they turn to the right or the left? Do they read every label? Do they look at every object? Etc. Etc. Every once in a while, spend a little time observing. Just walk around your museum as if you are a first-time visitor. At various museums, some of them my employers and clients, I have seen: trash on the floor, doors open to janitorial rooms, missing labels, a mop against a gallery wall, missing lightbulbs, etc. What do ticket buyers see?

In addition, find a little time to observe visitors in other nearby museums. Is the behavior the same there as in your museum? Share your stories of visitor service best practice with the rest of the staff.

Many years ago, I had the pleasure of learning from a board member who was a senior executive at Burger King. He talked about the importance of listening. "Don't worry," he said, "about people who complain. They are taking the time to try to make the experience better for themselves and for others. Worry about the people who are unhappy and just walk away. They are missed opportunities. You will never see them again."

The New and Improved Pyramid

Because most members will be found within the larger group of visitors, attracting visitors to your museum is an essential part of the development program. If we are going to raise money, we need to know our audience, why they are coming to us, and (perhaps even more important) why they are not coming to us. Are people who are very much like our current audience not coming to our museums because they don't know about us (a promotions problem), or are they not coming because they don't like what we do (a product problem)? Museum staff, boards, and committee members need to be out in the community, attending events and programs at other organizations, participating in service clubs, and talking, talking, talking to other people in order to get the pulse of reactions to your museum. Convention and visitor bureaus can be helpful, tourism cooperatives have a good sense of the out-of-town audience, hotel staff and cab drivers hear everything. Learn your market.

The goal is to expand the traditional thinking about where "marketing" ends and "development" begins. These labels artificially divide the staff members who are concerned about building relationships. That concern is traditionally reflected in a diagram as the development pyramid (figure 1.1).

In this model, from a large group of members, a subset of people will give to the annual fund. A subset of that group will give more substantial

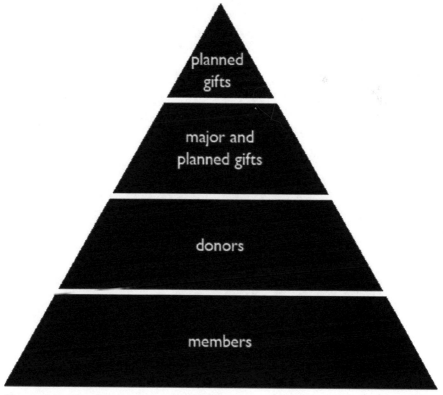

Figure 1.1. Typical Development Pyramid
Source: The Cornerstone Studio (East Hills, New York).

or major gifts. Perhaps a still smaller group will become donors to a capital campaign, and a much smaller group will become donors of portions of their estates in "planned gifts." This diagram is sometimes shown with arrows pointing from the bottom up to the top. The task of the staff in this model is to move people "up the pyramid."

We know, however, that the relation-building process begins much earlier than the membership program. The membership is a subset of a larger group composed mostly of visitors, and that group is a subset of our total marketplace, itself a subset of humanity. So rather than slice off the bottom of the chart in order to fit our usual job descriptions, how about a chart that looks like figure 1.2.

Again, we might augment this chart with vectors that indicate movement up from one layer to another. We know, in fact, that this kind of movement is not always true. For example, some of our best planned giving prospects

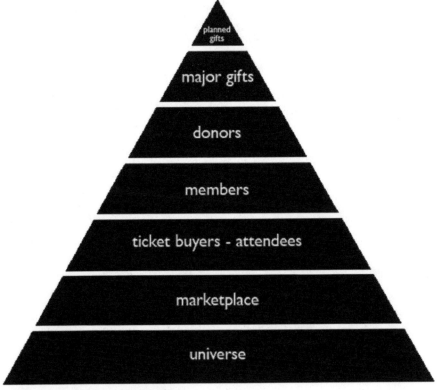

Figure 1.2. Expanded Pyramid
Source: The Cornerstone Studio (East Hills, New York).

may be volunteers who presently donate no money but give generously of their precious time knowing that later they may be able to leave something to our museums in their wills. So a chart truly reflective of our work may require lots of arrows linking each layer with several others, a messy prospect, but we're dealing with people, and people work is messy.

Because some of the people visiting your museum are likely to become members, gathering data about your audience—names, addresses, phone numbers, email—is an essential task. Some ways of accomplishing this task are to

- place a fish bowl or ballot box on a pedestal in the lobby, and ask visitors to complete a raffle entry form to participate in a weekly or monthly drawing for a catalogue or other museum item.

- ask attendees at lectures or other programs to complete a one-minute survey.

- use the survey as a raffle ticket for an inexpensive prize.

- conduct live intercepts with your museum audience. Carry a clipboard. Ask if they'd be willing to take a one-minute survey. (A volunteer can help with this.)

- capture names from charge card purchases in the museum store.

- run a mini raffle for participants in local organization group tours.

- ask visitor to sign in on a computer, like some free museums do (such as the Chemical Heritage Society and the Library Company in Philadelphia).

- add a mechanism on your website for online guests to sign up for your e-schedule or e-newsletter. You'll only have email addresses, but that's a start.

- start a guest book in your lobby so visitors can enter information and comments.

You may want to engage staff, docents, and other volunteers in gathering other demographic data. Many foundation proposal forms include questions about age, race, education level, etc. Amassing this kind of information will

SAMPLE ONE-MINUTE SURVEY

IMAGINARY MUSEUM OF CRAFTS

1. Is this your first time at the Imaginary Museum of Crafts? ☐ Yes ☐ No

   ☐ If yes, what led to your decision to attend today?

   ☐ Personal Recommendation ☐ News Story ☐ Calendar Listing

   ☐ Poster ☐ Mailing ☐ Social Media ☐ First Friday

   ☐ Other_____

   ☐ If you've been here before, what attracted you to return?

   _____

2. Have you visited other museums in this region? If so, which ones?

   _____

   _____

3. When you look for cultural information, do you seek it out by

   ☐ Newspaper   Which one(s)? _____

   ☐ Radio   Which station(s)? _____

   ☐ Television   Which station(s)? _____

   ☐ Web   Which site(s)? _____

   ☐ Social media (Facebook, Twitter, etc.) _____

   ☐ Other _____

4. What is your age? ☐ 16–22 ☐ 23–29 ☐ 30–39 ☐ 40–49 ☐ 50–59
   ☐ 60–69 ☐ 70 or more

5. ☐ Male   ☐ Female

6. Are you a collector of crafts?   ☐ Yes   ☐ No

7. Are you a collector of other art?   ☐ Yes   ☐ No

8. What did you see today at the Imaginary Museum of Crafts?

   ☐ Special exhibition   ☐ Permanent collection

   ☐ Store   ☐ Other _____

9. Which of the following best expresses your sense of the value of your experience?

☐ I would come back only if the museum was free.

☐ I would pay a small admission fee ($2–$3).

☐ I would pay a small admission fee ($2–$3) if an audio tour was included.

☐ I would pay a fee similar to other small museums in this region ($5–$10).

☐ The experience here is worth more than $10.

10. Would you like to know more about upcoming programs? If so, please complete this information:

Name_____

Address _____

City _____St._____ Zip _____

Email_____Phone_____

THANK YOU!

require other surveying techniques. Start with names and addresses and expand from there.

The Marketing Exchange

I have something you want. You have something I want. Let's make a deal, a marketing exchange.

In order to have a marketing exchange, five conditions must be met: (1) there are at least two parties, (2) each party has something that might be of value to the other party, (3) each party is capable of communication and delivery, (4) each party is free to accept or reject the exchange, and (5) each party believes it is appropriate or desirable to deal with the other party.

I give you something, and you give me something in return. It looks like this:

$$A \leftrightarrow B$$

What is the exchange that happens at a museum ticket counter? The museum is asking visitors to give money, and in exchange the museum is giving (choose one or all):

- the sense of well-being that comes from doing something valuable or educational.

- the chance to participate in something special.

- information not available to the general public.

- a lift to the spirits.

- escape from the everyday.

- access to individuals with knowledge and/or power and/or social connections.

- recognition, public or private.

- the good feeling that comes from helping others.

- access to our collections and our programs, etc.

Some museum staff may think that we are giving art, science, or history, but that "content" is *just one part of the exchange.*

The Development Cycle

Development is a process. First, we must identify our market. That market may begin as a large group of people, such as an entire community that is unfamiliar with our work, or it may be a single individual who has the capacity to transform our museum. How we proceed with the next steps will likely vary from one identified market to the next.

Our target market must be introduced to the museum. For many, this introduction will involve mainstream media, social media, and, for those who can afford it, direct mail. The link between what is usually called "marketing staff" and what is usually called "development staff" must be strong. If the market doesn't know about the museum and its work, it will not give.

Individuals must be cultivated. Special effort must be made to reach out to those who have interest and capacity. The largest community-wide market list is narrowed down through both formal and informal research. Even a quick Google of some names will reveal something about who gives where, who works where, etc. Who on your board knows people on your target list? Who can ask or at least can help pave the way for an ask?

The cycle looks like what is shown in figure 1.3.

1. Identify

2. Introduce

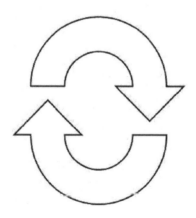

5. Steward

3. Cultivate

4. Solicit

Figure 1.3. The Development Cycle

Solicitation may be person to person, on site, by direct mail, etc. And then once a prospect has given or joined, the relationship is stewarded with a thank you note, encouragement to attend, new invitations, and whatever might lead someone to be a candidate for a next higher level of engagement and giving.

So the mature development program involves both advancing prospects through a cycle of relationship building and moving some prospects and donors up the pyramid. All of the processes of the pyramid and the development cycle are going on simultaneously and something like what is shown in figure 1.4.

The person responsible for development must have an eye on all of this activity, being as planful and intentional as possible so that prospects are advancing through the cycle and revealing themselves as potential donors of higher-level gifts.

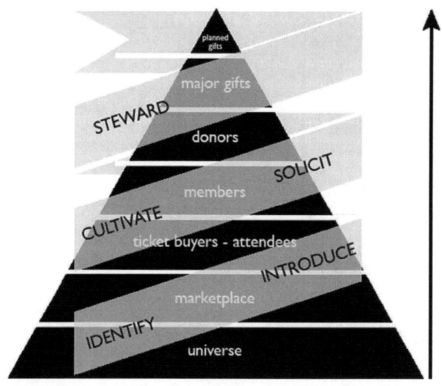

Figure 1.4. Combined Pyramid and Cycle
Yes, this is the sometimes messy and dynamic world of marketing and development. We are simultaneously identifying, introducing, etc., as a way to move prospects at different levels further up the pyramid. Source: The Cornerstone Studio (East Hills, New York).

Don't jump. In a small museum, the numbers of prospects at each of these stations of relationship-building may be small. The trick comes at the very beginning: be mindful of your market and choose wisely.

Donors: The Religious Motivation

Why do people give? Why do people voluntarily, of their own free will, dig into their pockets—or their checkbooks or their estates—and give some of their wealth to others?

When I've asked this question of audiences large and small, always among the first answers is "Taxes. To save on taxes." That answer does not make sense. If one's motivation is to save money, wouldn't one hold onto all of it? Why give away 100 percent so that you can save 27 percent (or whatever your bracket allows)?

Second, people have been making charitable gifts for quite some time, since way before federal tax forms and charitable gift deductions came into being. The idea has been deeply embedded in many societies for hundreds—even thousands—of years. Many religious texts encourage charitable giving. Here are some examples.

In Judaism, the central text, the Torah, includes numerous admonitions to remember the poor. The word "tzedakah" is sometimes translated as charity, but rather than being just a generous act, tzedakah includes the concept of justice and righteousness.

Maimonides, the twelfth-century Jewish teacher, rabbi, physician, and philosopher working in Morocco and Egypt, spoke of eight levels of charity:

1. The highest form of charity is to provide the means for a person to no longer be dependent on gifts from others. This kind of charity might be the creation of a job, instruction in a new skill, or provision of resources to start a new business, all given in a dignified manner.

2. Giving assistance in such a way that the giver and recipient are unknown to each other. In old synagogues, there was sometimes a little window where a gift could be left and another little door inside where the gift could be retrieved.

3. Donations when the donor is aware to whom the charity is being given, but the recipient is unaware of the source of the gift.

4. When the recipient is aware of the donor's identity, but the donor doesn't know the identity of the recipient.

5. When the donor gives directly to the poor without being asked.

6. When the donor gives directly to the poor when asked.

7. When the donor gives less than he should, but does so cheerfully.

8. When donations are made grudgingly.

In many Jewish homes, there is a tradition of a "tzedakah" box or "pishke," a place to put coins for charity, especially before the start of the Sabbath. Everyone is commanded to give charity, even those who are recipients of someone else's generosity, even the poorest of the poor.

The Bhagavad Gita, a central Hindu text, discusses three types of giving:

- A gift that is given without any expectation of appreciation or reward. Such a gift is beneficial to both giver and recipient.

- A gift that is given reluctantly and with the expectation of some advantage. Such a gift is harmful to both giver and recipient.

- A gift that is given without any regard for the feelings of the recipient and at the wrong time, so causing embarrassment to the recipient. Such a gift is again harmful to both giver and recipient. (Bhagavad Gita 17.20–22)

Any giving that is motivated by selfish considerations loses its value from the spiritual point of view.

Hindu philosophical texts such as the Isa Upanishad emphasize that true peace is found by adjusting our relationship to our possessions. We are not asked to renounce wealth, but rather to share it. Whatever we give will have no value if we part with our wealth reluctantly.

For Christians, charity is considered the highest form of love, a parallel to God's love for man demonstrated through giving as man's love of man. St. Augustine (354–430) wrote: "Charity is a virtue which, when our affections are perfectly ordered, unites us to God, for by it we love him." This emphasis on the goodness of charity appears often in the New Testament. A few examples:

- Hebrews 13:16: Do not neglect to do good and to share what you have, for such sacrifices are pleasing to God.

- 2 Corinthians 9:7: Each one must give as he has decided in his heart, not reluctantly or under compulsion, for God loves a cheerful giver.

- Acts 20:35: In all things I have shown you that by working hard in this way we must help the weak and remember the words of the Lord Jesus, how he himself said, "It is more blessed to give than to receive."

- Luke 6:38: Give, and it will be given to you. Good measure, pressed down, shaken together, running over, will be put into your lap. For with the measure you use it will be measured back to you.

Zakat, the third of the five central pillars of Islam, requires charity by every Muslim who is financially able. Wealth is recognized as a gift from God. Zakat is an obligation for those who have received wealth from God to respond by giving a portion of it to those in the community who are in need. The donor should not expect or demand any gains from the beneficiaries. Likewise, money should not be given with the goal of being recognized as a philanthropist. The feelings of a beneficiary should not be hurt, and the recipient should not be made to feel inferior for having received a gift.

From the Koran: "'Man,' said the Prophet, 'says: My wealth! My wealth!' Have you not any wealth except that which you give as alms and thus preserve, wear and tatter, eat and use up?"

Zakat has a particular emphasis on gifts that help the poor and gifts that release the bonds of slaves and debtors. In addition to this mandatory giving, Muslims are encouraged to make voluntary gifts to help those in need.

Numerous studies have demonstrated that "the more important religion is to a person, the more likely that person is to give to a charity of any kind" (*Chronicle of Philanthropy*, November 25, 2013).

No mention of taxes.

Is tax deductibility important to many donors and prospects? Yes, even with new 2018 tax laws. When appropriate, should you mention tax deductibility in your appeals? Of course. (For some gifts, it is required.) Is tax deductibility the reason someone is going to give to your organization rather than another? No.

Why Do People Give Today?

Too often, we assume that all people give to our cause because they are interested in supporting our mission. While this alignment of donor motivation and organizational mission may be true for some people, it is not true for all. Of all the many organizations that help the hungry, why do some donors support one and not the other? Why give to one local historical society and not the other? Why help one hospital and not the next? Surely, the choices donors make are not only about mission.

1. It feels good

2. They benefited from programs

3. Their children benefited from programs

4. To remember a family member

5. To honor someone

6. They have to give by law

7. It's good for their business

8. It's good for business in general

9. It's good for the community

10. A family history of involvement

11. They're in a position of importance within the organization

12. To respond to their social status

13. To acquire social status

14. To be among people with social status

15. To be among people with similar interests

16. They support the general purposes of your organization, although they don't benefit directly

17. To protect objects previously contributed

18. They are collectors

19. To preserve family history

20. For a tax benefit

21. To be among leadership businesses

22. To appear on a list

23. To have a name on a wall or building: legacy; immortality

24. To get more information

25. To keep connected

26. To join a friend in a pleasant activity

27. To meet people

28. To go to a good party

29. It is a religious value to give to charity.

30. They give out of habit

31. More

Donor Types

In their essential book *The Seven Faces of Philanthropy*, authors Russ Alan Prince and Karen Maru File suggest that there are seven types of donors:

1. The Communitarian: Doing Good Makes Sense

2. The Devout: Doing Good is God's Will

3. The Investor: Doing Good is Good Business

4. The Socialite: Doing Good is Fun

5. The Altruist: Doing Good Feels Right

6. The Repayer: Doing Good in Return

7. The Dynast: Doing Good is a Family Tradition (Prince and Maru, 14–17)

What is the range of motivations among your donors? What are their different needs? The formal party that is perfect for one type of donor does little for another. The wall signage that recognizes one type of donor is inappropriate and undesirable for another. How can your development program serve all the different needs of all the different donors you have and those you seek?

You may wish to create a grid, identifying the donor motivations and the piece of your program that fulfills the various donor needs.

Table 1.1. Work Chart to Meet Donor Motivations

Kind of Donor Motivation		Possible Offering	
Socially motivated	Annual gala	Cocktails at home	
Civic stalwart	Annual report listing	Board/committee role	
Business investor	Wall signage	Annual report listing	Networking event
Up-and-coming leader	Networking	Young donor group	
Long family tradition	Meet in person	Twenty-five-year donor group	
Mission aligned	Lectures	Meet service recipients	Behind-the-scenes tour
Etc.			

The point is to make sure that somehow the different kinds of donors are getting what they need.

All of this discussion about motivation and needs leads us to understand that the process of making a gift is very much a classic marketing exchange. Or perhaps it is better to say that we have a number of different types of exchanges going on simultaneously.

Actions Speak Louder Than Words

We live in an age of superlatives, where every product is "The Best, The Fastest, The Cutting Edge, World Class." How can this be? How can every car be the fastest? If just about every museum is world class, then that qualifier means very little.

What about the slogan "the best in the region?" Sometimes, taking a cue from political gerrymandering, museums define their region in a way that allows them to be "the best." "The XYZ Museum is the largest science museum in eastern Washington County (if you don't consider any of the cities)." "The ABC Museum is the largest art museum between East Nowhere and West Podunk."

Don't talk about superlatives. Be the superlative. Be sure that your visitors have extraordinary experiences every day. Provide exceptional service every day.

Fill your museum with people. Nothing promotes the sense of quality than a crowd. Local people will assume that if the museum is good enough for "other" people then it is good enough for them.

If your goal is to create a crowded museum, of course you will want to advertise. You will use every medium your budget will allow: TV, radio, newspapers, online, social media, word of mouth. These days, many potential visitors (even the locals) turn to online sites to read the endorsements of other visitors. Why not ask your board members to post their reactions online? And ask others close to your museum.

Another strategy is to work with other noncultural nonprofit organizations to provide discount tickets for their constituents. Senior centers, after-school programs, neighborhood associations, camps, and other social service agencies often serve populations that might not regularly visit museums. Invite them in. A discounted ticket, rather than free admission, gives the experience some value. Often foundations will help fund these special audience experiences. Annual fund donors will understand and appreciate your efforts at outreach.

Other museum visitors will see a crowd. Like travelers on an airplane, museum attendees do not know who paid full fare, who paid a discounted fee, and who came for free. What they know is the feeling of success: "My, that place was busy."

Your mission may say that you serve the people of a certain region. Serve them. All of them. And serve them well. Everyone benefits.

Who Gives?

Perhaps you have noticed that the emphasis so far has been on individual giving. This emphasis is intentional. Although the media gives much attention to huge gifts that come from time to time from huge foundations or corporations, in the United States most giving comes from individuals.

Each year, the publication *Giving USA* tracks trends in national giving. In the data released for 2015, a summary of all giving to all nonprofit organizations reports that 71 percent of gifts came from individuals. An additional 9 percent of gifts came in the form of bequests from individuals. By contrast, 16 percent of all giving came from foundations and only 5 percent came from corporations. Similar data were reported by the Philanthropy Roundtable. Although there have been occasional dips, the overall trend has been an increase in total individual giving since 1975.

The message is quite clear: focus on individual giving.

Another not so positive message extracted from the numbers is that of all giving in 2015, only 5 percent went to arts, culture, and humanities organizations. Museums compete with theaters, orchestras, dance companies, lecture series, and other cultural activities for a relatively small slice of the giving pie. The largest percentages of gifts went to religious and education institutions.

The Philanthropy Roundtable also reports that 73 percent of the revenue for all nonprofit organizations comes from fees for service. These fees include tuition, merchandise sales, tickets, etc. Transactions are the most important part of the revenue equation.

Marketing: Selected Additional Resources

Beckwith, Harry. *Selling the Invisible: A Field Guide to Modern Marketing.* New York: Business Plus, 1997.

Bergeron, Anne, and Beth Tuttle. *Magnetic: The Art and Science of Engagement.* Washington, DC: AAM Press, 2013.

Durham, Sarah. *Brandraising: How Nonprofits Raise Visibility and Money Through Smart Communications.* San Francisco: Jossey-Bass, 2010.

Levinson, Jay Conrad, Frank Adkins, and Chris Forbes. *Guerilla Marketing for Nonprofits.* Irvine, CA: Entrepreneur Press, 2010.

Mokwa, Michael P., William M. Dawson, and E. Arthur Price, eds. *Marketing the Arts.* New York: Praeger, 1980.

Peters, Thomas J., and Robert H. Waterman, Jr. *In Search of Excellence.* New York: Harper & Row, 1982.

Peters, Tom, and Nancy Austin. *A Passion for Excellence: The Leadership Difference.* New York: Random House, 1985.

Pine, B. Joseph, and James H. Gilmore. *The Experience Economy.* Boston: Harvard Business School Press, 1999.

Prince, Russ Alan, and Karen Maru File. *The Seven Faces of Philanthropy: A New Approach to Cultivating Major Donors*. San Francisco: Jossey-Bass, 1994.

Giving USA
Philanthropy Roundtable
Center for Advancement of Informal Science Education
Smithsonian Center for Education and Museum Studies
Visitor Studies Group (UK)
Visitor Studies Association

TRANSACTIONS

How wonderful it is that nobody need wait a single moment before starting to improve the world.

—Anne Frank

Membership and Value

When some of America's oldest museums were founded, membership had a different meaning from the one commonly applied now. In the nineteenth century, the members of some museums were, in fact, voting members of the corporation. Those members had direct responsibility for the management and financial stability of their museums.

Today, most museum members feel only some responsibility to show up every once in a while so that they are getting full value from the money they paid in advance.

From time to time, a finance person, perhaps a member of the board, will ask, "Is membership worth it?" When all of the elements of a membership program are factored—that is, staff time, printing, postage, events, etc.—there may be little net revenue. But just like the same question about a special event, membership must be regarded as part of the larger development plan and as part of the museum's community engagement plan.

Just within the membership area, the relatively high cost of new membership acquisition in year one is offset by the relatively low cost of membership renewal in year two. In addition, we can apply our average annual renewal rate and know that many of our members will have a very long life-span. If we accept the idea of a development pyramid, then, for many people, membership is the gateway to other forms of giving, especially to the annual fund. While some museum membership programs produce net revenue, for many museums, membership is the equivalent of the retail "loss leader."

For museums that receive public funding or are situated on public land, museum members can be important and vocal advocates.

The commitment to attend, inherent in the value proposition made by many members, produces attendance for exhibitions and educational programs. In addition, museum members may bring along others who are not members. Many of these attendees will shop in the museum store (perhaps for a small members-only discount), eat in the café, register themselves or their children for classes, or send their little ones to the museum camp. In that light, membership is not only "worth it," it is essential to the life of the museum.

Benefits: The Membership Offer

Your ticketing offer, usually free general admission for a year, is the center-piece of your membership benefits program, but other benefits should be added to your menu to entice others and to make the value proposition even stronger. Remember that people give for a variety of reasons; your membership benefits should touch those who seek information, socializing, exclusivity, networking opportunities, etc.

Your basic menu might include:

- Members-only exhibition previews.

- Members-only lectures or tours or discounted special programs.

- Discounts in the museum store (including online store) and café.

- Extra guest tickets. Often these are used by out-of-town guests who are unlikely to join.

- A special members-only admissions line or window. This is valuable if your museum is very popular.

- Complimentary audio guide.

- Invitation to an annual gala. (Note this is not free.)

- Discount on catalogues or other publications.

- A subscription to a newsletter or quarterly publication. ("Knowledge is power." [Sir Francis Bacon] It also is your chance to sell upcoming programs, exhibitions, and merchandise, and it provides a vehicle to acknowledge donors and sponsors.)

- Members-only hours.

- Discounts at nearby restaurants or stores.

- An annual report in print or online.

- A special gift.

- Opportunity to join a special interest group within the museum, such as the Contemporary Art Society, the Young Professionals, or the Sky Watchers.

- Free use of the library and archives.

Not all of these benefit ideas will be possible or appropriate for every museum.

For families, groups of two, or households, these benefits are offered to multiple people at a higher price. Some museums offer senior memberships at a discounted rate. Other museums know that since so much of the audience is composed of seniors, a special discount does not make financial sense. In addition, they know that many of the seniors who join have enough disposable income to afford the full individual rate.

At the next levels of membership, sometimes called patron, the benefits begin to shift from the mostly financial/value-oriented to more exclusive opportunities to engage those people who choose to give a little more. These memberships move beyond the purely transactional toward more relationship. It is likely that this group will be small enough that you can meet most of these members. Benefits might include private tours with curators, exclusive dinners, and travel with the museum director to other cities. Each of these benefits has a social value for the members and, given the smaller size of the higher-level membership group, a better chance for staff to get to know these members on an individual basis.

At the highest levels of membership, an extra ticket or a bigger discount probably has little value. If a member can afford $1,000 a year to join, that member likely can afford an extra $10 for an additional ticket. What can the museum give to these good and generous members that money cannot buy? Some ideas include:

- Use the museum staff's personal contacts to arrange travel to places these members could not see on their own: behind the scenes at another museum, a private collection, an architectural gem not open to the general public.

- Social gatherings at the best homes, hosted by the best people.

- Private salons with special guest speakers.

- An annual black tie dinner.

Many museums find that their membership skews older. To attract a younger demographic, some museums have created young professional groups that highlight networking opportunities. As in other nonprofit organizations, many people who join these groups want not only to give but to volunteer as well. They seek meaningful use of their time. These volunteer opportunities may overlap with other programs already in place; it is likely you are using volunteers to help organize a special event or two or to serve as docents. You may try to channel the young professionals' energies into these existing programs, but they may want to work and socialize among themselves. Some museums that began young members groups in the 1990s and 2000s found that these members were *too* demanding of staff time, and the programs were dropped. If you have the resources to create this membership program within a program, why not do it? But remember that your time is your most precious resource.

Many museums are eligible to participate in reciprocal benefits programs. Members who join at a certain level or above receive free admission to similar museums in other parts of the country. Among these reciprocal programs are:

- North American Reciprocal Museum Association

- ASTC Travel Passport Program

- Association of Children's Museums Reciprocal Network

- Modern and Contemporary Reciprocal Program

- AZA Reciprocal Admissions Programs

In addition, some of the regional and/or statewide museums associations provide reciprocal benefits opportunities.

Finally, every member gets a thank-you. With a goal of making sure that your first-year member gets the sought-after value, use the acknowledgment as your first reminder of what special exhibition or program is coming up next. Welcome them into the family. Tell them that you hope to see them soon. In addition to a note, ask your board, your development committee, or other volunteers to follow up new members with a thank you phone call. Even if most of these calls reach answering machines, your new members will be impressed.

Membership Acquisition

Members are enlisted through a number of means. On-site recruitment is essential, for it is while they are in the lobby that visitors are calculating membership value. These visitors want to get their money's worth, so they must believe that they are going to come back. Just like the coming attractions in a movie theater, your lobby and your visitor services/ticket-selling staff must help you promote the promise of the future visit: exhibitions coming soon, exciting programs planned, and upcoming promotions in your shop. Development and visitor services staff must know about it all.

If you are enjoying particularly large crowds, use staff or volunteers to "work the line" by offering the chance not only to get dollar value but to save precious time by getting out of line for service at a special membership station. Even better, use technology to complete the membership and ticketing transactions right online.

Direct mail is a good way to reach large numbers of people, especially when a new special exhibition is about to open. Emphasize the promise of members-only previews or special events so that members enjoy something the general public cannot. While some museums make this offer through a mailed brochure, numerous tests have demonstrated that the most effective mailing devise is a packet that includes an outer envelope with an alluring message, a letter highlighting the special exhibition and extra benefits, a response card, and a reply envelope. Member benefits can be listed on an addition card or insert. Because many homes are bombarded with mail offers, make yours stand out by design, by a special discount offer, and by a cutoff date. If your offer can be used any time, it is more likely that it will be used at no time.

Especially when a special exhibition is coming, you can take advantage of the enthusiasm of your board, your volunteers, and your staff. Challenge each board member to enlist a few members. Provide an incentive for volunteers who help recruit new members: an extra ticket, a guided tour, etc. If you have many volunteers, form teams with captains, subgroups, and workers and offer (donated) prizes for the team that sells the most, for the individual that recruits the most, etc. If this effort involves enough people, seek a business, perhaps the exhibition's corporate sponsor, to fund the entire competition.

Large museums acquire members through telemarketing. An outside firm is hired, and professional callers (sometimes well-trained, sometimes not) make sales calls. The costs are relatively high, and with the increasing use of caller ID and answering machines, these phone efforts are more difficult.

Many potential visitors will come first to your website. A prominent tab should lead these visitors to membership information. While it may be easier and seem more secure to accept payment through a third party, this process often leads the potential member away from the museum's messaging and into a bland sign-up form. Try to do it on your own.

Who are you asking? Because no museum can reach every household in its market area, the list must be focused down. As you think about lists, consider the demographics of your current constituents. Your next members will be similar to your current members. What lists lead you toward those similar households? Do your trustees or other volunteers have personal lists you can use? You might be able to borrow or exchange lists with other cultural or educational organizations. You might gain access to lists of civic champions through service club membership lists. You might notice that many of your members live in just a few zip codes; you can mail to everyone else in those communities. The subscriber lists of certain publications might match closely with your demographics. Whichever lists you choose, be sure to cross reference ("de-dupe") so that your current members do not receive a new member solicitation and so that other prospects receive only one mailing or call.

However you choose to recruit new members, your promotion must be aligned with your other marketing activities. For example, while the focus of the direct mail campaign may be to enlist members, that promotion also will entice some people "just" to buy a ticket, giving you the on-site opportunity to discuss membership. You and the entire museum staff are in this together.

Membership: Renewals and Upgrades

Wouldn't it be great if all people acted the same way at the same time? Then we would know exactly how to respond. In the real world, members have many different kinds of behaviors. In part, these differences are because we have encouraged them to join at different times of the year and at different levels. We have asked them to join us for a year of discovery, and we must respond as the year of discovery comes to a close. In short, renewal of members must be scheduled on cycles that correspond to the months when members enrolled or last renewed. There is just no way to "lump several months together to save time" or to "do it just once or twice a year." Sorry.

Renewal notices should be as personal as possible, referring to the past year's level of membership. The renewal is your chance to remind members of the fabulous year that is closing and to let them know what is coming up. There is no need for a fancy brochure; they already know you. The packet can be a simple letter, a reply card/form, and a return envelope.

A renewal cycle should include multiple reminders. These current customers are your best customers, and after a few years you will know that 60 or 70 percent or more will renew at a cost much lower than the beautifully designed and more randomly sent acquisition mailing.

If, for example, you are planning a cycle of three renewal mailings, a first reminder should be sent a month before the membership expiration date. The purpose of this mailing is to entice. A secondary purpose is to encourage an upgrade to the next highest level of membership. Perhaps all upgrading members can be invited to a special gathering. Hold out that carrot; some members will bite. If someone does upgrade, write a little note on the acknowledgment letter: "Thanks for the upgrade."

The second mailing has a more urgent tone. Surely they don't want to miss all the excitement. The third mailing, skipping the upgrade appeal, should not come down too hard. Surely no one wants to feel like a "deadbeat." Assume they forgot about it. This is a gentle reminder.

Some people will not renew because they have moved or their life circumstances have changed. Some people simply forgot. Some people were unhappy with their first-year experience. The only way to know who is who is to ask. This can be done with a brief online survey that not only asks for their comments but also serves as yet another gentle reminder.

Unless you know that they have left the area or passed on, keep these nonrenewal names on your prospect list for the next big mailing. Perhaps they do not like Civil War exhibits, but they are eager to attend something about colonial quilts.

Business Members

Many business owners can justify gifts to the museum only if they help their marketing objectives. These objectives likely include greater visibility and networking opportunities. A small museum might consider a business membership category with different levels of giving and benefits, such as:

- Website listing

- Annual report listing

- A decal or certificate of membership/support to hang in a public place

- Free tickets

- Opportunity to purchase additional discounted tickets for clients or customers

- Opportunity to purchase discounted museum store merchandise

- Invitation to an annual business friends night, a networking reception

- Discounted facility rental for a business meeting or reception

Target businesses include companies associated with present and past board members, collections-related businesses, vendors, businesses that want to reach the museum's core demographic, small businesses on the rise, civic champions, etc.

Business gifts may be a special component of your annual fund, with different levels of giving related only to different degrees of recognition. This group can be led by a cadre of business volunteers who engage other business leaders in the outreach effort. The achievement of the annual business goal can be touted among the business members and others in your various publications.

Corporate Matching Gifts

As a way of encouraging philanthropy by their employees, some companies provide matching gifts, sometimes called "workplace giving." In most cases, the company will match dollar for dollar a gift made to a nonprofit organization. Sometimes these matches are restricted to a certain geographical area, close to the company's base or bases of operation. Sometimes these matches are restricted to a certain kind of organization, such as health or education. Often corporate matches include gifts to museums. Generally, the companies have a maximum amount they will match, cumulative gifts up to $1,000 or $2,500 or whatever. A few very generous companies match two for one!

The responsibility to securing these dollars rests with the employee. Most matching gift companies have a form the employees must complete and submit to their human resources (HR) officer or finance department. Occasionally those forms will require a confirming signature from museum staff.

While you cannot decide which companies are going to choose to offer matching, you can help to promote the idea by including a check-off box on membership, annual fund, capital gift, and other of your museum forms:

☐ This gift will be matched by my company _____.

This is an easy way to remind your members and donors that this company benefit may be available.

In addition, in your newsletter, quarterly, and/or annual report, list all of those companies that have matched gifts to you. Such listing not only reminds the employees of their benefit but also nudges another company to consider this idea.

How does your museum account for this matching gift? Is it recorded as a gift from the employee, or is it a gift from the member or donor? Although the matching gift check (sometimes for multiple members or donors) will come from the company, this match is a benefit the employee can choose to send your way or not. This company benefit is part of that employee's hiring package, just like time off or health insurance. The employee—rather than the HR director—is deciding to share that company benefit with you. I recommend adding that match as part of the total employee contribution. If the employee joined as a member with a check for $50 and the company sends a match for $50, the member is now listed at the $100 level and receives museum benefits at the $100 level. The member's acknowledgment letter should recognize that the gift came in part from the company. And the matching gift company should receive an acknowledgment as well. (Because some companies may have many employees participating with you, you might send these company acknowledgments once or just several times per year, listing all the employees whose gifts were recently received.) In addition, as noted earlier, the company should be listed wherever gift lists appear as a matching gift company.

How do you know which companies in your region will match gifts to your museum? Check out donor lists for colleges and hospitals nearby. Call the HR offices of all the largest companies in your area (a good volunteer or intern project). Check online sites such as doublethedonation.com. Start promoting the idea of matching gifts, and informed employees will tell you about programs at their companies.

Sponsorship

Back in the day, in many small and midsized communities, many companies had a sense of giving back to the communities that helped them grow. Often company founders were born or raised in the community, and it was likely that family members or descendants of the founders continued to be civic leaders. Sometimes we continue to see the names of founding families, many of them collectors, on museum labels. Unfortunately, much of that sense of civic responsibility is gone. Companies have merged with other companies, leadership has been acquired from across the country or around the world, and the relationship that founding families had with museums has been lost or greatly limited.

Yet many companies understand that connection with the region's museum may be good business. The museum's constituents, generally educated and with higher than average household income, are just the kinds of people sought after by banks, insurance companies, luxury car dealers, wealth managers, and the makers and sellers of high-end products and services. For these and similar companies, linking the corporate name to the museum brand is a good marketing decision. For most companies, sponsorship has little to do with philanthropy and more to do with sales. Decisions about potential sponsor dollars are usually made by marketing staff, sometimes with a strong nudge by a senior corporate leader with an interest (perhaps as a member of a board or a committee) in art, history, or science.

Sponsorship is about a classic marketing transaction. (In some museums, the task of securing sponsors resides with marketing rather than development staff.) The company gives dollars, and the museum gives visibility. Everyone wins. (Occasionally this relationship is disguised in the form of a grant in which, after standard grant questions about mission and project, the applicant is asked to discuss how the project will be promoted and where the "funders" name will appear.)

In addition to background information and lots of pictures about the exhibition or program for which sponsorship is sought, the sponsorship proposal should emphasize:

(a) Audience. How many people are projected to attend? What does the museum know about them? Age? Zip codes? Education? Media habits? What has the museum learned about its market from surveys or from readily available demographic data? (b) How will the company's name/logo be used? It is helpful to be as specific as possible: How many ads and where? How many posters? How many brochures distributed and where? All of this adds up to a number of *impressions*, times the corporate name/logo will be seen and heard.

For example, the company name and/or logo will appear in/on:

- Print ads

- Brochures and flyers

- Social media

- Media releases

- Outside banners

- Entry to exhibition

- Quarterly publication

- Annual report

- Invitations

- Billboards

- Exhibition catalogue

- Exterior signs and kiosks

- Posters
- Press kits
- Media preview invitations and kits
- Front and/or back of tickets

And the company name will be mentioned:

- Opening night comments by director
- Welcome comments by staff at lectures and programs
- Radio ads
- Audio tours

And there will be special opportunities:

- Preopening tour with curator
- A number of guests at opening event
- A private cocktail event/dinner
- A number of tickets for program/exhibition
- Free admission for all employees (and families)
- Merchandise discounts

And there may be product placement opportunities, such as a chance to give out a "swag bag" with a company brochure as guests leave the opening night party.

These benefits and others like them should be arranged so that sponsors at a lower level (likely for a smaller or less popular project) receive fewer impressions than the sponsor of the next international blockbuster.

Some exhibitions or projects may be so big that multiple sponsorships are needed. One way of doing this is to have tiered sponsors, such as platinum, gold, and silver. Another way of recognizing multiple sponsors is to break the full project into smaller pieces so that there is an exhibition sponsor, an education program sponsor, an audio tour sponsor, etc.

Surely not every museum has the capacity to provide all of the recognition opportunities listed here. Some museums may not buy ads or use billboards. Do what is right and possible for you. In addition, *in advance of seeking sponsors*, create some policies about what is and is not allowable for you. Will the corporate name go above (XYZ Company presents . . .) or below (Sponsored by . . .) the exhibition title? Will product placements be permitted? What kinds of discounts maintain at least a break even situation in your gift shop? Who gets to speak where and when? Are there recognition standards in your community? If other cultural institutions nearby are giving sponsors the sun, the moon, and the stars, you may have to as well.

Finally, in addition to all of the thank you notes, a benefit you might offer is the advanced opportunity to learn about upcoming exhibitions and programs. There's nothing like a satisfied customer to be your next customer.

Tributes

Many years ago, my mother spent her final days at a small hospital on Long Island. Despite the best efforts of the doctors and the extraordinary compassionate care she received, she passed away. My mother had lived in Florida for quite some time, and I was living in Massachusetts, but I was so impressed by the care she had received that my wife and I made a small gift to the hospital, a tribute in memory of my mother.

Tributes are gifts made in memory or in honor of someone. In museums, that someone may be a member of the board or staff, a volunteer, a docent, a friend in the community who benefited from a museum program, a civic leader who recognized the value of the museum, or the tribute may be made in honor or in memory of a family member or friend of anyone connected to or impacted by the museum. Sometimes just a single gift may come to the museum, perhaps a way someone in the community chooses to honor a graduation, an anniversary, or a special achievement. At other times, perhaps on the death of the museum's founder or a beloved longtime curator, a hundred gifts may arrive. These gifts are random, often onetime transactions, and often from people the museum does not know. The donors may not even know the museum.

Promotion of tribute gifts involves regular reminders. Include tributes as a giving option on your website. Encourage those close to your museum to make tributes in honor or in memory of those people they love. Ask them to consider listing your museum in their wills as a place where memorial gifts might be sent. Include a tribute form in your printed materials such as your quarterly. Such a form should:

- provide an option to choose whether the gift is sent ("In honor of . . ." or "In memory of . . .").

- include a fill-in space for who is being honored or remembered.

- include contact info for the donor.

- include contact info for the person being honored or a family member of the person being remembered.

Follow up the tribute with a thank you note to the donor as well as an acknowledgment note to the person honored/family of the person being remembered. This acknowledgment should not include the amount of the gift.

A year after I made the tribute, I received an annual fund solicitation from the hospital where my mother died. I received a similar letter the following year. My mother died twenty-five years ago and, although I have not made a gift since the original tribute, I am still receiving solicitations. This seems unreasonable and a waste of the hospital's dollars. The point is that the relationship between a museum and many of its tribute donors will be thin and short lived, generally limited to a single transaction. These tribute donors need to be coded so that those people who live far away from the organization's market area and who are not giving now should be dropped from the mailing list.

Special Events

The CEO of the regional office of a huge national nonprofit organization knew that something was wrong with the organization's special events. Could I attend the next one and observe?

That next event was a thank you affair for donors of fifteen years or more. By definition, the guests were older. Many were elderly. They were invited because their long history of giving led staff to believe they were good planned gift prospects. The evening consisted of several brief speeches, some entertainment, and a dessert reception.

Several hundred guests had preregistered for chartered buses, which came from multiple points in the large metropolitan area. Others would be coming by car. Still others would likely just show up.

What I observed was extraordinary staff energy spent on making sure that the event ran smoothly. Most of the staff had "been through this before," and they awaited the guests with some anxiety. Wait, wait, wait . . . and then all of the buses seemed to arrive at the same time. Hundreds of people left their buses simultaneously and approached the long reception hallway. Each of the guests had to be registered on the way in and then given a name tag. The staff, seated behind the registration tables, arranged in two parallel lines, was overwhelmed for perhaps fifteen minutes. Then many of the guests needed assistance with seating.

In advance of the speeches and the show, the board chairman took it upon himself to walk up and down the aisles, greeting and thanking guests. In front of the large room, several people, including the CEO, were involved with a group photograph. I recognized a couple, extremely wealthy, to whom nobody spoke.

The entertainment was fine and the brief speeches were on point. The dessert reception was lovely. The guests expressed their gratitude as they left the reception hall for the buses, with extra desserts and some mission-related brochures in hand. The staff went home exhausted. This special event was a good example of a development team losing its way. So much energy was focused on the logistics that some of the basics of good development work were forgotten. Those basics, noted earlier, apply to special events, too.

- Identify

- Inform

- Cultivate

- Solicit

- Steward

A fundraising event provides opportunities to advance each of these stages of development work. We must continually talk to people, interest and inform them, and excite and involve them in our mission.

Sure, a brochure can do some of the work, but, as noted by the Center on Philanthropy's "Ladder of Effectiveness," a person-to-person conversation filled with information and enthusiasm is the best form of fundraising.

If you've organized a special event such as a gala, an auction, or an annual ball, you've probably heard some of the critique from your board even before the event was over. "What a load of work!" "Is it worth all the staff time?" "We only made X dollars?" "Should we do this next year?"

A "successful" event is typically defined as one that made a lot of money. Perhaps it's not the event that needs to change. Instead, you may want to redefine "success."

Surely money needs to be part of the equation, but that is just a part. Think of your events as pieces of your comprehensive development program. In addition to your financial goals, set specific goals for introducing new people to your organization and for stewarding relationships.

What if you and your team said that through your event you were going to reach out to one hundred new prospects? Because of that goal, your staff and your board/volunteers have the assignment to comb through their contact lists so that one hundred people who have never before been invited to one of your events now receive an invitation. Perhaps every board member, staff member, and volunteer has the assignment of suggesting two or three names. Then they have the assignment of reaching out to the new invitees. Then, at your event, they have the assignment of saying "Hello" to those new prospects—their contacts—who accept the invitation. Suddenly, your event is about something other than—or in addition to—just money. Now you are focused on bringing new people closer to your leadership and your mission. Afterward, during evaluation, you should be able to say, "Not only did we raise money, but we identified our targeted number of new prospects for follow up about deeper involvement." *That* is success! Another opportunity: during your event, be sure that someone has the responsibility to greet and thank each of your most important donors. In some cases, this responsibility might be a simple acknowledgment of past generosity or an additional short comment, such as, "We hope we can count on you for continued support." If the donor says "Yes," follow up the event with a confirmation letter. If the donor says "No," follow up with a call to find out more. These chats are brief. Most important, they are not left to chance; they are assigned conversations. At your evaluation, discuss what happened. "We had forty-two conversations with our donors. Forty of them confirmed their plans to renew their annual gifts." That sounds like success!

A special event provides numerous touch points for person-to-person conversation. For the event described above, I first suggested placing energized staff members on the buses—to greet the guests, to handle some of the checking in procedures, and, most important, to talk about the good work being done. Here are some more ideas:

Checking in

- At the beginning of an event, place the CEO or board chair near the check-in area. That way he or she will have a chance to say hello to just about everybody.

- Instead of a row of volunteers or staff being seated behind a table, why not have them stand in front of a table so they can more easily talk with the guests. Or you could try a podium, to look like the maître d' station at a restaurant ("Oh, Mrs. Jones, so nice to see you! I have your table assignment right here").

Cocktails

- Ask a staff member or volunteer to be on the lookout for guests standing by themselves. It is hard to come to a large event as a "single." Make sure these guests feel welcome.

- Avoid placing all the food tables against the walls. A table of dips in the middle of the room encourages conversation.

- Provide each board member with background on two other guests who should be greeted during cocktails.

- While the event described here did not have cocktails, there was a period of time when many guests were seated in chairs, waiting. Why not assign staff members (or board members) to various sections of the room to give thanks and simply make conversation. When I was waiting, I spoke to the person next to me, an older gentleman. I learned that he had no children, was grateful to the host organization for years of service, and wanted to "do more." Imagine if such simple conversations had been organized throughout the crowd!

Seated dinner

- Place a senior staff member, a board member, or a key volunteer at each table to serve as a table host, with responsibility for introducing guests at the table to each other and for making a short toast: "Here's a brief toast to all of you at table six. Thank you for

45

your support of the XYZ Association. Through your generosity, we're able to do so much good work. Cheers."

- Use place cards. Make sure staff, board members, and volunteers are seated next to people you want them to get to know.

Dessert

- Informal passed desserts can provide another opportunity for circulation among the guests.

- A round table with a tray of chocolates near the exit provides a way to slow the departure as well as another opportunity for conversation.

Exit

- Make sure someone important is near the door to say "Thanks for coming!"

In short, examine your event for every moment that encourages person-to-person engagement.

The kind of schmoozing that will engage a donor or prospect does not come naturally to every CEO, staff member, or volunteer. The chief development officer (CDO) has a responsibility to help all the players prepare for their event roles. Included in this responsibility is writing sample scripts for table toasts, providing background on everyone at the table, and making sure that the CEO, board chair, and other members of the team have clear assignments, with suggestions on language that can be used ("Sam, I'd like to give you a call next week to talk about a project I have in mind"). In many ways, it is like choreographing a dance: every moment of the event should be carefully thought out.

Then, after the event, the CDO is responsible for debriefing (gathering the little shreds of information that were collected, like the man in my example who wanted to "do more"), reminding everyone to follow up on the calls to "Sam," the thank you letters, the "good to meet you" notes, etc.

For this to work, in addition to raising money, the cultivation and stewardship roles of your special event must be clearly identified up front as goals. Early buy-in is essential.

Your next special event does not end when the guests go home. Think of the event as the beginning of numerous cultivation opportunities for new and deeper relationships. And yes, the logistics must be perfect too.

The party may be over, but the development work has only just begun.

This essay is based on an article I wrote for the NonProfit Quarterly, *"Realizing the Full Potential of Your Events" (January 12, 2012).*

Special Events: Part Two

Each spring, Winterthur Museum, Garden, and Library, the historic Delaware home and property of Henry Francis du Pont, hosts its signature fundraising event, Point-to-Point, featuring horse racing, elaborate tailgating, fine dining, and multiple other indoor and outdoor activities. The odds are that your small museum lacks the extensive acreage, volunteer corps, horse country enthusiasts, and staff to organize and manage something quite so special.

If you want to organize a special event, where do you start?

You might begin by looking at your mission, your community, and your constituents. What can your museum do that cannot be done by anyone else? Yes, others might be hosting special dinners, but what do you have, what knowledge, what objects as starting points, what talents that cannot be found elsewhere? What in your museum's history can help you both raise money and raise pride? Was the founder well known? Does your museum celebrate an ethnic community? Are you all about kids? The answers to these probing questions can lead you to a unique way of shaping and presenting your event.

Most events fall into one of these categories:

- Annual gala (dinner, dinner and dancing, honoring somebody)
- Auction (wine, silent auctions, antiques, goods and services)
- Guest performance (music, dance, lecture, followed by reception)
- Golf/tennis/sports tournament
- Craft, art, or antique show/sale
- Run/walk
- Raffle

- Season opening (cocktails, music)

- Fashion show/luncheon

These ideas are not mutually exclusive. For example, a wine auction may be preceded by a dinner with the vintners, then a wine tasting, then the auction, including a raffle for a visit to vineyards in Italy. To make your event financially successful, think about multiple streams of revenue. These might include:

A. Corporate sponsors. Most fundraising events are designed to attract people of wealth. Who wants to reach that market? High-end car and other luxury product dealers. Investment and finance advisors. These businesses are willing to pay to reach your prescreened audience. For many events, all the upfront expenses are covered by these sponsors.

B. In-kind. Are there portions of your event expenses that can be donated? For example, a local florist may not be able to give you cash, but she may be able to give you centerpieces. Likewise, you may be able to secure donations of music, food, linens, parking for guests, A/V systems, theater lighting, use of an off-site space, etc. Some museums have been able to broker a deal with food wholesalers who donate raw food that is then cooked by the caterers.

C. Individual sponsors. Some people will pay more in order to meet with a celebrity, sit at a better table, gather in advance at a wonderful home, or have their names listed. Often an honoree will make a special gift to the museum.

D. Vendors who will pay for a space where they can sell their wares.

E. Raffle sales, silent auction, etc. Perhaps your centerpieces are donated by local crafters or other vendors; then they can be auctioned.

F. Ticket sales.

Some of the work can be done by volunteers, but staff must remember that your volunteers are likely to want to attend. (Yes, they should pay.) They are your prospects for other gifts, too. You must work hard to make sure that they are successful and that they are recognized for their success among their peers.

Communications

The tasks associated with communication in museums are not easy ones. The tasks of communicating with members are even harder.

Acting on the theory that value-seeking members and/or their families who come to exhibitions and programs are more likely to renew, we want to encourage attendance and participation. Typically, much or most of a museum calendar or quarterly publication has content related to upcoming opportunities to participate: the next exhibition opening, the next lecture, the next class. Here's how to register. Here are all the dates you need to know for the next few months, "so plan now." Sometimes I see a "Letter from the Director," clearly not in the director's voice and simply a summary of all the titles and dates that follow. Too often the story copy is very close to the copy used in a media release, the who, what, when, and where.

Rarely do members hear about the why. Why is this important? What is the point of view? What can they know as members that nonmembers will not know? What should visitors (members) seek out? In short, how can staff add more value to its communications with members? Alongside the basic information about the next project, why not add an interview about the project with the curator or educator in charge? Or an interview with the exhibit designer or the registrar? How can we pull back the curtain on a project to empower our members with a behind-the-scenes glimpse of the most important activities? Why not a suggested reading list of books or recent articles on the topic? Knowledge is power.

The task of communicating with members, however, is far more complicated. If we go back to the idea of a pyramid, we also want to encourage our members to think beyond the ticket price value level, so that those who have the means become donors. To move members beyond the transactional, we must inspire them with those mission-related activities that they may not know or see. Sometimes these are the quiet but influential activities that are funded by foundations or government agencies. These mission-related activities might include funded school tours for certain nonparticipating populations, research of the museum's collections that will become part of a book or a national study, collaboration with the region's social service agencies, or special opportunities for visitors with disabilities. These kinds of stories introduce the idea that the museum is more than just a place for casual visits. It is likely that your museum is a force within your community, perhaps a force for social change, perhaps a source for economic growth through increased tourism, or perhaps a force for new education partnerships with colleagues who serve seniors, preschoolers, or others who are often left out or left behind. By including these messages in your regularly scheduled membership communications, you pave the way for increased giving to your annual campaign. As New York clothier Sy Syms used to say in his ads, "An educated consumer is our best customer."

Of course, another way your museum increasingly communicates with your members is through your website. Just as in your traditional printed materials, be sure there is a place for mission-related information. (In addition to your members, you will enlighten all those foundations that ask on their proposal guidelines for your website.) Instead of hiding your good work three tabs down under "About," why not headline your mission work with words like "The Museum in the Community."

Social media provides many opportunities to promote your organization, but it is perhaps more useful for short-term event or program information. One small museum sends out a brief message each week about a single object in the collection. Another museum sends me LinkedIn messages on everything from exhibition openings to programs to "Did you know?" items about the collections or related topics to social opportunities nearby. I sometimes receive five or six such messages a day. I don't read any of them. I get overloaded. Just because social media is easy and inexpensive does not make it good for *every* message.

Another way to communicate the full menu of mission-related activities is to craft a special communication to a select group of your constituents. This group might include upper level members, your board (most of whom should be upper-level members), foundation heads, or government and civic leaders. The communication can be relatively simple in the form of a special letter that will come from time to time from the director to let these most important people know what is going on behind the scenes. The first time I tried this, I drafted a letter about what happened behind the scenes before my museum presented a "blockbuster" exhibition. I wrote about the years of planning, the efforts to secure key works from other institutions and private collectors, the research team, the costs of shipping and insurance, etc. Truly, most visitors see objects on a wall or in cases and have no idea of the work, beyond a few nails, that goes into bringing a project together. Surely the readers of that letter did not know. Some of the readers wrote back to me to say, "I didn't know." Some of the readers sent checks.

Make your mission count from the very beginning of your constituency relationship. If the only things you emphasize are tickets and prices, that's all your members will think about, too.

Transactional Giving: Selected Additional Resources

Allen, Judy. *Event Planning: The Ultimate Guide to Successful Meetings, Corporate Events, Fundraising Galas, Conferences, Conventions, Incentives and Other Special Events.* Hoboken, NJ: Wiley, 2008.

Mandell, Terri. *Power Schmoozing.* New York: McGraw-Hill, 1996.

Rich, Patricia, and Dana S. Hines. *Membership Development: An Action Plan for Results.* Gaithersburg, MD: Aspen, 2002.

Rich, Patrica, Dana S. Hines, and Rosie Siemer. *Membership Marketing in the Digital Age: A Handbook for Museums and Libraries.* New York: Rowman & Littlefield, 2015.

Americanmuseummembership.org

CHAPTER THREE
GIVING TO MISSION

It's easy to make a buck. It's a lot tougher to make a difference.

—Tom Brokaw

Annual Fund

Openings. Parties. Tickets. For some of your constituents, these social benefits will not be meaningful. Some people simply want to support the good work of your museum, or they want to be sure that more people have the opportunity to participate in your good programs. The annual fund is a vehicle for unrestricted giving. The full gift goes to support the work.

Sometimes, if there is no other explanation, "supporting the work" might be interpreted as paying for the day-to-day operational costs of the museum. A few people might understand the full range of your administrative needs, but for most people, giving to the museum so that pads and pencils can be purchased or electrical cable connected does not conjure up images of meaningful work being accomplished. So it is helpful to focus those images on the special beneficiaries of your good programs: children, disadvantaged neighbors, seniors, etc. Such focus will touch the hearts of civic champions. If you use language such as "supporting the educational work of Our City Museum," much of what you do—school programs, public programs, interpretation of any kind, publication—can fall under the "educational work" umbrella. That's not quite 100 percent unrestricted, but it is very close.

SAMPLE ANNUAL FUND APPEAL LETTER

XXX

XXX

XXX

Dear XXX,

In autumn, my favorite color is yellow.

Yellow is the color of school buses. I love to see them lined up outside the museum because it means we're doing our job. When I see children in the gallery, I know that the James A. Michener Art Museum is fulfilling that part of our mission that promises to offer "a diverse program of educational activities that seeks to develop a lifelong involvement in the arts." That word, "lifelong," means we must start with the very young.

In 2006, the museum provided group tours for 5,758 students. More than 4,500 students participated in Art on the Move, a program so innovative it was recently recognized with a rare second grant from the Institute of Museum and Library Services. Additionally, 1,394 teachers benefited from teacher programs and in-service classes. Surely, the museum is an important and well-used educational resource for our region.

Our commitment to lifelong learning also includes adult programs, such as lectures, gallery tours, First Fridays, concerts, and films.

Although some of these programs are offered with little or no admission fees, they do cost money. Our exceptional cadre of curators, educators, and presenters must be paid. Curriculum and project materials are expensive. Pre-visit classroom packets and activity kits require design, copying, and mailing.

Yes, we're doing our job. We're doing our job well because of the continued generosity of friends like you. With gifts—large and small—from those who support educational excellence, we are able to teach, to engage, and to inspire.

The arrival of those yellow school buses in the fall also means that the end of the tax year is close at hand. Won't you consider a special [additional] end-of-year gift to the James A. Michener Art Museum? Your tax-deductible support at this time will help us reach even farther and provide even more for students of every age.

On behalf of all who seek a lifelong involvement in the arts, I thank you.

Sincerely,

Courtesy James A. Michener Art Museum

Many museums rely on direct mail to promote gifts to the annual fund. The mail response is bolstered by stories (with gift forms) in your publications and by phone calls. Some people will be members and annual fund donors, while some folks will choose one or the other. The kinds of questions about net return to the museum that sometimes dog membership programs will not come up for the annual fund. Managing the annual fund is very low cost, and most of the revenue goes directly to the museum's bottom line.

The annual fund is more focused on your mission. Donors to your annual fund are aligning themselves with your mission, moving from a more transactional relationship to one that is more relational.

Membership and Annual Fund: How Often?

I volunteer at a food pantry. Each week, between 120 and 160 people come to fill their bags with donated food. Although they are asked to take only so much of each item—one produce item, one bread, etc.—sometimes a "client" will ask for an extra. "Please, sir, may I have an extra can of sardines?" "May I take just one more tomato?" These folks are needy, and they are appreciative. The volunteer work is extremely rewarding, and I have become an advocate for food sustainability. In addition to my time, I have donated some money to the pantry.

This is not my first food-related cause. Because of the involvement of one of my friends, I made a donation to another, much larger, food distribution nonprofit. A few days later, I received a nice thank you note, and included with the note was another request for money. "Okay," I thought, "these people are committed to a cause, and they are not shy." I made another small gift. I got another thank-you and another request. In fact, the requests kept coming, every two or three weeks. After a while, I decided that if they could spend so much money on direct mail, they didn't really need my next small gift. After a year or so, they stopped asking. No one called to ask why my gifts had ceased.

How often is too often to ask? In a membership program, it is common to send a request a month or two before the annual renewal date, then a request around the renewal, and then a reminder a month or so after the membership has lapsed. Three or four asks, each with a slightly different message. If a member at a higher level has lapsed, a volunteer or intern might call with one final reminder. Then, the next cycle, I would send a brand new membership request and start the process from scratch.

Your annual fund program—your solicitation of gifts more purely for the work rather than for the benefits—should have a different rhythm. Perhaps you have a fall campaign and a spring campaign. The advantage of this split program is that you can solicit annual fund gifts off cycle from membership renewal. So if a member's renewal comes up in October, you can solicit an annual fund gift in April. This will be far less confusing than receiving multiple requests for multiple kinds of gifts in a compressed period of time.

The annual fund usually works more around your schedule than the donors' schedules. One year you may solicit annual fund gifts in November, while the next year, because of the opening of a major exhibition or the launch of a huge program, you might move annual fund solicitations forward or backward. Your first mailing should reference past gifts: "Last year, you helped with a generous gift of $XXX. Please consider a small increase this year so that we can help even more children." "In the past, you've helped with a gift of $XXX. . . ." A second letter should reference past giving as well. Then try a phone call. Then try a final letter asking for a gift of any size.

Some advisors (especially in your finance department) may suggest you keep on mailing as long as the cost of the mailing gets covered by responses. Yes, your museum can ask more than once, but do not badger your members and donors. Constant asking becomes annoying, and you risk losing a friend.

Perhaps the large agency with the nonstop mailings got the message. Starting a year or so ago, they began sending just one request to me each year. But now, I give to my little food pantry. They appreciate my gift. They respect my time. I think they use my money wisely.

More Annual Fund

I started my career in the professional theater. When I switched into non-profit theater management, I found that most people understood that the tickets they purchased benefited themselves. Most often, the single ticket buyers and the subscribers sat in "their" seats. A small number of people, however, said they were "supporting" the theater by attending. (I guess they would say that they "support" Macy's or Burger King or whatever by buying.)

Museums have a more complicated relationship with their audiences, and in some ways we (the museum professionals) have created our own confusion. In museums, buying tickets, generally at a low price relative to the performing arts, is not enough. We ask people to become members. The members sometimes forget that in exchange for their higher dollar purchase of a membership versus just tickets, they are receiving a host of benefits: special programs, discounts, etc. Then we confuse them further by encouraging upgrades to higher and higher levels of membership. In some museums, one can be a member at the $1,000 level, the $2,500 level, the $5,000 level, and beyond. At what price point does the membership become less about getting benefits (the transactional relationship) and more about "supporting"?

Now, in addition to whatever generous checks have been written, the museum starts thinking about an annual fund. First, we turn to our most likely and informed market—our members—and ask for a gift. Surely many of these members, especially at those high levels, must feel that they already have made a gift.

How do we distinguish one relationship from another? Some thoughts:

1. Try not to use the word "support" in membership appeals. Especially at the lower levels, membership is about benefits for the member.

2. You might say, "Membership is about you enjoying everything the museum has to offer. The annual fund is about helping others." "Membership is your gift to you. Through the annual fund, you make a gift to others."

3. Because some people feel that giving to the operating fund buys only pencils or paper, you might define something other than "general operating" as the designation for annual fund gifts:

    a. Support the museum's mission to serve the community/region.

    b. Support the work that goes on behind the scenes.

    c. Support our school-based education programs. Support our outreach.

    d. Support the opportunity for those in our community who cannot afford to attend.

4. Suggest levels of giving, and then suggest what a gift at each level "buys": "Your gift of $100 allows a class of twenty students to attend." "Your gift of $500 helps conserve one work on paper." "Your gift of $1,000 allows an entire grade from an inner-city school to enjoy a planetarium program."

5. While in many museums, memberships, especially at the lower levels, are tracked by the bookkeepers as earned revenue, the annual fund is all about philanthropic giving. Usually, the only benefit annual fund donors receive is recognition. Recognition may include:

   - Listing in the quarterly or other regular publication

   - Listing in the annual report

   - Listing on lobby signage

   - Listing on the website

   Another form of recognition I have tried is an honor roll, a printed list of donors (separated by giving levels) that is inserted into the first annual fund appeal mail packet. Through this inexpensive vehicle, all past donors see their names in print, and they know that others see their names in print along with their giving levels. It is subtle. It works to encourage increased giving.

6. Make the financial case, especially after a "blockbuster": "It is easy to be deceived by popularity. The large numbers of people who come to the museum, and the ticket revenue and the program registration fees they provide, do not—and cannot—cover all of the expenses of running a museum like ours. Our mission is to serve the entire region, so we must keep our fees low and affordable."

7. When soliciting members at the highest levels, let them know that their membership includes their annual fund commitment. They will not be solicited twice. However, send them a sample of the annual fund appeal packet with a note: "Although we promised you that we would not solicit you twice, you may hear from some of your neighbors that they received something from us. We just wanted you to know what is going on." Despite your promise, some higher-level members may choose to give more if they know the way the additional money will be directed.

8. Thank you. Thank you. Thank you. Of course, a gift acknowledgment needs to be sent quickly, and the same matching gift procedures that you use for membership apply here. In addition,

if annual fund gifts are enabling something special to happen, let the donors know: "Because of generous people like you, we have been able to . . ."

Many museums install a donation box near the exit. If you do this, include a mission-related message, such as, "Your donation supports the conservation and care of our collection. Thank you." You won't accumulate a huge amount of money this way, but you will start to plant the seeds of philanthropy just as visitors are feeling positively about their museum experience. Experiment with additional locations for donation boxes, too.

Communication continues to be the key. As people move up the pyramid from being members to becoming donors, or for people who visit or know about the museum but skip the membership step altogether, promoting the museum's mission becomes more important. Especially in museums with higher membership turnover, such as science and children's museums, communicating the mission, outreach programs, and behind-the-scenes research will encourage some people to keep giving or to start giving, even when the interest of their children/family wanes.

How Many Campaigns?

Many years ago, there was a TV ad for prunes in which viewers were asked, "Are three too few? Are six too many?" The delicate question of "Too few or too many for *what*?" was never asked.

Some museums question whether they should have both a membership program and an annual appeal. The answer for a smaller museum sometimes depends simply on the available labor. Membership requires acquisition, delivery on a menu of benefits, and renewal. Some of the benefits, such as discounts at the museum shop, may have real costs that reduce the net revenue return to the museum. However, because they have those very same tangible benefits, memberships may be easier to sell. The annual fund is typically simpler—the benefits are usually various forms of recognition—but with its emphasis on mission, the "value proposition" may be more abstract.

Some people will support both initiatives; they will become members and give a little more. Others may give just to the annual fund. For example, someone who had a long-standing family business in your community but now spends much of the year elsewhere may feel that the opportunity for free tickets or discounts will never be used, but they may still want to support their hometown museum. Older, past board or committee members may want to continue to help "their" museum even if they cannot be present physically. Some people are "civic champions," people who do not necessarily get excited about history, science, or art but who understand the economic and social value your museum provides to the region.

If you can, do both. With their different messages, your membership campaign and your annual fund campaign will call out to different people. Each program brings groups of people onto your donor pyramid, likely prospects for other kinds of participation and/or giving.

The Shortest Essay: Board Giving

Increasingly, foundation and corporate funders are asking (sometimes on a proposal cover sheet) how many (or what percentage) of your board members make a financial contribution to your museum.

Increasingly, sophisticated individual donor prospects are looking at the various lists you publish or hang on your walls, and they compare the list of board members with the lists of donors. Who is giving?

The question prospective funders are thinking is, "If those most responsible for the future of this museum are not giving, why should I?"

The answer simply must be that 100 percent of your board is giving to your museum, most at the highest levels.

Explanation of the expectation of board giving is a task of your nominating committee. Be clear at the very beginning.

Major Gifts

Like the expression "One man's floor is another man's ceiling," what counts as a major gift in one museum may be quite different from a major gift at another museum. In some museums, the category of "major gifts" includes all gifts of some level and above. At a very small museum, that level may be $250 or $500. At another museum, major gifts may start at $1,000 or $2,500 or more. Sometimes major gifts include the highest membership levels.

In addition, there are likely times when your museum will need a special onetime infusion of cash in order to bring an exhibition or program to fruition. Again, at some level and above, these special gifts may be considered major gifts.

Whatever your definition of major gifts, what may be most important is that some group of your most generous donors gets your extra special attention. That attention may be special recognition, special invitations, or special access to your director or curators. Somehow you have determined that these donors have both the capacity and the interest to make a major difference for your museum.

"Capacity and interest" is the key.

Occasionally at a committee meeting, some well-meaning friend will ask, "Why haven't we approached Bill Gates?" Or substitute Oprah Winfrey or another billionaire. Yes, we know these people have huge capacity, but do they know that your museum exists? And do they care? Often the "interest" part of the formula is far more important. There are many stories of people with relatively modest means making gifts larger than might have been anticipated because the museum—your museum—is an essential part of their lives.

A great way to start to understand capacity and interest among your constituents is to host a confidential rating meeting. Invite eight or ten people who know your community or your audience from different points of view. These should be people who travel in different circles and who are involved not only with your museum but also with other organizations. To this group, you will bring a list of names. The list surely should include all the highest-level donors to your museum as well as those currently giving at the next few levels down. Add to the list your most loyal volunteers. Add the names of top donors to nearby or similar organizations. And add the names of leaders you've heard about in business journals or through other media. At your rating meeting, discuss each name. What is known? Here are the kinds of things you might hear:

"Yes, Sally is loaded, old family money."

"We've tried for other causes. The only thing they care about is golf."

"Jim is fantastically wealthy, but his wife is seriously ill."

"Jack has all the money. Jane collects Chinese sculpture."

"Sam is my brother-in-law. Don't bother."

"Mary is a great prospect. I see her at bridge club every Tuesday. I should invite her to something."

"Peter is moving to Timbuktu."

"They certainly have the means. Has anyone asked?"

"They just built a new house in Tahiti. They're at their place in Paris now."

"It's all show. They don't have much."

The result of a couple of hours of chatter (some might say "gossip") is that you now know quite a bit about where to spend your time and where to pass. For some prospects, you may have the beginnings of a strategy . . . Chinese sculpture . . . golf outing . . . someone knows Mary. And you know who has money but is never going to care. (Some people just do not have charitable intent.)

Another kind of prospect research happens online. Because many organizations publish annual reports or donor listings on their websites, you may try a "Google search" on your prospects. You may find that some prospects give small gifts to a wide range of organizations. You may find that some prospects make huge gifts to their colleges but give little elsewhere. You may find that a prospect serves on a committee at another museum. These all are pieces of a puzzle.

Similarly, ask your board and/or development committee members to share with you playbills, programs, annual reports, quarterly magazines, etc. These are good research tools to discover who is giving what where. When you visit other organizations—museums, theaters, private schools, hospitals, any large civic group—look for a donor listing in the lobby. Again, you may see a name or two of interest.

A number of private companies provide "wealth screening" services. For a fee, these companies will search all public and other records to create profiles of a list of donors. Some of these services provide a score for each prospect, matching data about capacity (value of home, publicly traded equity, boats, etc.) with known giving history. You might then match this screened data with the prospects' giving history to your museum. If you have a branch of the Foundation Center nearby, or if your local and/or college library subscribes, you can do some of this work yourself. But as with other development work, time is money.

At the end of this research, you should have a list of best prospects. Anyone identified as a best prospect should have a well-conceived strategy that leads to a personal ask.

Major Donor Benefits

What do you give the person who has everything? Sometimes this question comes up for birthdays, maybe Christmas, perhaps Mother's Day or Father's Day. Does the person who has everything really need another tie tack or a new bud vase?

What do you give the person who has everything and who gives some of it to your organization? Most organizations are fortunate to have among their constituents people of significant wealth who donate substantial amounts of money. How do we acknowledge this generosity?

In too many organizations, the most generous donors are acknowledged on a continuum of benefits that begins with those who give small amounts. In museums, the lower levels of giving are often grouped into a membership program. In museums that charge an admission fee, entry-level members generally receive free admission as a benefit. Sometimes members at a slightly higher level receive a free pass or two. At an even higher level, members might receive three or four tickets. What about at the highest levels? If one can afford to give $5,000 or $10,000 or even more on an annual basis, isn't it likely that the donor could easily afford the next $15 ticket?

For these highest-level donors, what can we give that money can't buy? Here are some thoughts:

1. Treat these donors to opportunities to meet your people. Lunch with your most senior staff will result in a more informed and more engaged donor.

2. Arrange meetings with other leaders in your field: guest curators, visiting scholars, the author of the latest book in your field, political advocates for your cause.

3. Use your professional connections to provide access to places not usually open to the general public. These places might be your own (collections storage, research lab) or elsewhere (behind the scenes at a major medical facility, backstage at the symphony, soon-to-be-opened group home or halfway house).

4. Provide opportunities for your major donors to meet each other. Perhaps a generous donor will invite others for cocktails or brunch. Or perhaps the executive director invites small groups of donors for tea in her/his office.

5. At one-on-one meetings with the executive director, ask their opinions. Share some thoughts about the future and elicit their responses.

6. More.

The point is to create a program that moves from benefits that are transactional (tickets, tote bag, newsletter) to those that are relational. Respond to your highest-level donors by becoming more generous with your information, your connections, and your time.

You are the benefit that money cannot buy.

SAMPLE FORM 3.2

SAMPLE SPECIAL LETTER

March 20XX

Dear Friend,

The Accreditation Commission of the American Alliance of Museums recently informed us that the XYZ Museum has met the highest standards of the museum field and has achieved reaccreditation.

Only 10 percent of multidisciplinary museums like XYZ are accredited. Out of more than 21,000 museums in the United States and Canada, only 1,048 are accredited. Only 38 museums in our state are accredited.

Accreditation is based on Characteristics of Excellence encompassing all areas of museum management and operation. The accreditation process is centered on self-study and peer review and takes eight to sixteen months to complete, every ten years.

Among the many areas of review are:

- Mission
- Governance
- By-laws
- Planning
- Code of ethics
- Human resources
- Development
- Exhibition design/fabrication
- Exhibition research, curation, and interpretation
- Conservation
- Security
- Facilities management
- Public relations
- Marketing
- Legal counsel
- Membership
- Collections management
- Finances: detailed breakdown of sources of revenue and expenses

In addition, the museum had to meet national standards for Core Documents, including Institutional Plan(s), such as a Strategic Plan; Collections Management Policy; Borrowing Policies; Institutional Code of Ethics; Emergency Response and Disaster Preparedness Plan. Other plans reviewed by the Accreditation Commission included our Collections Plan, Conservation Plan, Interpretive Plan, and our General Facility Report.

As you can imagine, the package submitted for national review, several hundred pages of documentation, required considerable input by many members of our professional team.

After all of these plans, reports, and answers were approved, a two-person team of national reviewers visited XYZ Museum for several days, meeting with senior staff and touring through all corners of our facility.

Our formal notice of accreditation arrived just a few days ago, and, of course, we are thrilled.

But credit for success does not go just to the staff. Your leadership and your support, along with the participation of so many other friends, members, donors, volunteers, and advisors, helped create a picture of XYZ Museum as an essential part of the cultural and educational fabric of this region. Through you, we continue to receive national recognition.

Thank you so much for helping us achieve reaccreditation. We are very proud.

Sincerely,

Ms. X

President and CEO

Planned Gifts

Planned giving is a catch-all name for the various ways that donors can make a gift to your museum as part of the distribution of their estates. Generally, this distribution occurs after the donor dies, but there are a few legal ways a donor can give you money now and still reap considerable tax advantages later.

For most donors, however, tax advantages have little to do with why they might leave money to your museum. As noted much earlier, if they really wanted to "save" money, they wouldn't give anything to anyone. In addition, many if not most planned gifts to the museum will not come from your wealthiest contributors. Instead, people who feel close to your mission and to your work, but who may not be in a financial position to give now, may find it attractive—a way to extend their interests beyond their lives—to give later. This means that the marketing of planned gifts needs to be broader rather than restricted to just the upper tier of your donors. This is a case of some prospects skipping over several layers of your "donor pyramid" in order to do something substantial. A prospect may be living a very modest life, with Social Security an important piece of the household income. Now the donor can give the museum only a modest membership each year. In addition, this donor donates time as a docent. Later, the "modest life" prospect leaves behind a small house valued at several hundred thousand dollars, a few pieces of jewelry, and some cash. Because of your museum's lifelong relationship with the prospect, some of that modest estate can come to your institution.

While there are several legal and financial vehicles that allow donors to make planned gifts, most such gifts—some estimates are as high as 90 percent—will be in the form of simple bequests via the donor's will. From their various colleges and universities, some of your donors may be aware of other ways to make an estate gift, but these very large institutions, with thousands of new alumni each year, have very large pools of prospects. It is likely that your prospect pool is much smaller. So if your development staff is just yourself, or perhaps you have just a few other colleagues working with you, don't get too bogged down in the legal and financial nuances. First of all, you probably are not a professional financial advisor and should not be giving financial advice. Second, you probably won't face the complicated questions of, for example, a charitable lead trust versus a charitable remainder trust.

You don't need to have all that information at your fingertips; you can create a structure to get the information to those few planned giving prospects who might need it. Here is how:

- Create a folder or a library of planned gift materials from colleges and universities, just to have on hand.

- If your area has a Community Foundation, meet with the executive director. Community Foundations offer a range of advisory services to donors. They may be able to help you, too. Surely they will have information. They may be able to steer some prospects your way. They may (in exchange for a fee that is likely smaller than someone else's fee) help with investments and reporting.

- Create a small ad hoc committee of planned gift advisors. This group might include three or four professionals, such as an estate lawyer, a life insurance agent, and a trust officer. The group may meet just once a year, but they are in the wings if a donor has no idea where to turn.

- Ask this group to assist with developing language a prospect might use to create a bequest to your museum. This language will be just a sentence or two.

- If you are writing about planned giving, whether a brochure or a short article, ask this committee to review the language.

A planned gift has a sense of permanence, and prospects are more likely to give in this way if your museum has been around for a while, has a sense of financial stability, and has staff and board leadership that is steady and respected. If yours is a new museum, planned giving is not the place to start.

A bequest may be unrestricted or restricted. An unrestricted bequest can be used for the general purposes of the museum or for something specific, as you choose. A restricted bequest can only be used in the way the donor intended. Be sure to encourage your prospects to speak with you before they sign on the dotted line. You don't want to be in the situation of receiving a gift that hampers your work or that is restricted to uses beyond your mission.

Bequest language can be as easy as this:

I give and devise the sum of _____ dollars (or x%) to the Small Museum, Inc., a nonprofit corporation located at 321 Main Street, Smallville, IN 998765, tax identification number XX-XXXXXXX, to be used for its general purposes.

A simple bequest is relatively easy, but so is procrastination. Many prospects do not want to confront their own mortality, so they do little or nothing to plan for the future. A Harris Poll survey conducted in 2015 revealed that 64 percent of Americans do not have a will. One of your essential development tasks is to remind your constituents often to do the right thing for themselves and for your museum. Every issue of your quarterly should include a short article, just a few paragraphs, about bequests. When there is space, include the specific language approved by your ad hoc committee.

Include a similar feature in your annual report and include a tab under your "Give" or "Support" tab on your website. Once a year, work with your CEO and board chair to put the subject of planned giving onto the agenda for a board meeting, and follow this up with a survey asking if any of the board members have estate plans for your museum. Ultimately, the constant reminding will lead to some questions and then to some plans.

Make a special effort to reach out to your docents and to other volunteers. By giving generously of their time now, these people are giving a strong message about their interest.

Survey as many of your members as you can afford to do. Once you have knowledge of a handful of people who have planned gifts for your museum, share with them the idea of a legacy society. One of the benefits of such a group is a listing, with the donors' permission, in your publications of their names. You might also host, or (better) have a member of the society host, an annual get-together such as a tea or a morning coffee in which some plans or dreams for the future are presented by the CEO.

Occasionally, someone close to your museum will bequeath an object, perhaps a painting or a historic document. The museum's collections committee should include guidelines in the collections policy about what may be accepted into the collections and which objects will be given to other institutions or sold. Even rarer will be a bequest of real estate. Work with your development and finance committees to consider in advance how you will deal with this kind of gift.

As your program matures, in time you will receive a legal notice that your museum has been included in the will of a deceased member. Soon after, you will receive a check. If you know the family of the deceased, thank them. Thank the lawyers or other professionals involved with getting this gift to you.

Grants

I have served on several grant review panels. In each case, many of the proposals under review were poorly written, filled with grammatical errors, and simply unclear. Some prospects submitted proposals after the published deadline. Some prospects did not include the required attachments. Grant reviewers said, "If the organization doesn't care about what it is submitting, why should we?" Some people with responsibility for grant preparation and submission should be fired.

Many foundations are created by individuals or families as vehicles for their personal giving. Support from such foundations generally follows the same sort of identification, information sharing, cultivation, solicitation, and stewardship that you use for individual prospects. These are individual prospects; they are just paying with one checkbook rather than another.

Other foundations have more formal structures. Although they may have been created by an individual or a family, they now have a board that has grown beyond or replaced the original donors. These foundations often have websites, guidelines, procedures, and deadlines. As with the case of the panels on which I served, decisions about who gets what money are sometimes made by people totally outside the foundation board and staff, sometimes from outside the community or region in which the foundation is giving.

These "private" foundations are the focus of this essay. In many ways, government agencies that provide grants are like these foundations: by law, they have to give away their money.

Ten Commandments for Successful Grants

1. Research. Board members (and some other well-meaning people) will occasionally ask why the museum is not receiving money from the Most Generous Foundation. Fortunately, a number of sophisticated resources are available for research into who is funding what, so that you might inform the well-meaning people that Most Generous only makes grants in Wyoming, and we are in New Jersey. Or you might learn that the foundation only gives money to colleges doing research on health issues in Africa.

    Among the best and often easiest resources is the Foundation Directory Online. Your museum can purchase a yearlong subscription at relatively low cost. Much of the information is available online for free. Even more of their information may be available at your local library. You can enter terms like "Museum," "Arts," or" Omaha" to begin a list of foundation prospects.

    Foundations with annual budgets of $25,000 or more are required to file a federal 990 form. These are available for free at Guidestar. com. In the filing, you will find the names of foundation trustees, the amount given annually, and (most often toward the end of the document) a list of who received how much money in the filing year.

These lists provide a framework for your request. If the foundation's largest previous gift was $5,000, your museum should not ask for $50,000.

If your region has a community foundation, that CEO will likely know quite a bit about your foundation prospects. Likewise, your board members, volunteers, and colleagues may have knowledge about who is doing what. While you are chatting with others, enlist their help to create a collection of annual reports from other organizations.

Finally, many opportunities are listed by the American Alliance of Museums, state arts councils, and professional organizations.

2. If possible, talk with the funders. Someone runs the foundation, perhaps as CEO or perhaps as a clerk. That someone may meet with you. Surely there's no harm in an introductory email or phone call. Add that person to your mailing list so that he or she is regularly informed about what your museum does. In addition, there may be opportunities through a community foundation, local arts collaborative, Association of Fundraising Professionals, or other organization to "meet the funder." Go. Ask a question so that you have a chance to introduce yourself. Reintroduce yourself at the end of the program.

3. Apply where there is a "fit."

4. Follow the instructions. If the limit is three pages of narrative, don't send four.

5. Use compelling language. "We need help to solve a problem." Organizations don't have problems/challenges. People do. Your museum exists to serve some public. (It probably says so in your mission.) So what does the public need now? For example, "In order to meet the demand for hands-on history learning by elementary school teachers in our county, the XXX Museum is requesting $XXXX from the XXX Foundation." How do you know there is a need? Have you conducted any studies? Have others conducted any studies?

Simultaneously, be careful with superlatives and unsubstantiated claims like "world class" or "highest level." According to whom? Mention validation your museum has received from outside sources, such as, "The evaluator from the state arts council, Mr. X, said . . ." "For two consecutive years, the museum has received a letter of commendation from ABC." Or create your own validation by engaging your marketing staff (or part of your own marketing time): "We regularly evaluate public programs with audience surveys. Sixty-two percent of our program attendees say that our lectures are "the highest quality." Answer who, what, when, and where. Is there research that validates the methodology? Are there individuals on staff especially prepared to do this work or will you bring in consulting experts? Who are these project leaders, and what in their experience will help them be successful with something new?

6. <u>Answer: Why this? Why now?</u> Does this build upon earlier work? Is this an essential piece of your strategic plan? Is this a response to an audience need that has recently surfaced? In short: How is this project the logical next step for your organization?

7. <u>Demonstrate capacity to be successful.</u> If you've done something similar, or similarly complicated, let the readers know.

8. <u>Match the budget to the proposal.</u> Be sure that every action mentioned in the proposal is included, even if the anticipated cost is zero.

9. <u>Find impartial readers.</u> What is clear to you may not be clear to someone else. Test your proposal before you submit it.

10. Follow up:

    a. YES

        i. Thank you. (We will list your name as _____ ,)

        ii. Share your success. Let funders know how well their dollars were put to use.

        iii. Invite them.

    b. NO

        i. Call to see if you can have a conversation about improvements you can make for the next round. Solicit critiques (if they are not included in a rejection letter).

ii. Listen to critiques.

iii. Continue to communicate about your organization's good work.

iv. Invite them.

Most private foundations lay out some sort of process for submitting a proposal. They may have an online application. Generally, if something about the process is not clear, there is some way to contact the foundation for information.

Some foundations provide no guidelines other than limiting your request to two or three pages. In this kind of informal application, include the following, most of which was mentioned earlier:

☐ We need help to solve a problem.

☐ A full description of the problem to be addressed.

☐ Project description.

☐ Brief history of your museum, especially how your museum is uniquely capable of providing a solution to the problem (you have the expertise or you will get the expertise).

☐ How this project fits into your plans? Context.

☐ Evaluation plan: What will success look like? How will you determine if you've reached your benchmarks?

☐ Outcomes. Definitions I see more and more:

  • Outputs: the work that is done, the specific tasks. (We will bring four hundred school groups to our museum for a special program.)

  • Outcomes: What has changed because of this work? (We will demonstrate that they've learned something, that writing has improved . . .)

☐ Budget (sometimes as an attachment). Budget must match your story. Have you allocated money for all you need?

☐ Other commitments already received.

☐ Conclusion: with you as a partner a critical need will be met.

On one grant panel, a fellow reviewer, feeling overwhelmed, said, "Everyone has put a lot of work into their proposals. Everyone should get funding." Ah, if that was only possible in the real world. Foundations have limited funds available, and some foundations are besieged with proposals. As a way of narrowing the field of viable requests, many of these foundations have introduced a preliminary process, the letter of intent (LOI). Occasionally, this step involves a few simple questions about your organization and the project for which you will apply. Sometimes, the LOI is as complicated as a full proposal. Follow all the guidelines mentioned here. The foundation is looking for ways to make its decision easier. Don't allow your museum to be dropped from contention because you left something out.

To help you through your year, create a schedule arranged by submission deadline (table 3.1). If there is no suggested deadline, create one for yourself. Share the schedule with staff and board.

Table 3.1. Foundation Schedule Worksheet

Foundation	Notes and Attachments	Submission Deadline	Date Submitted	Expected Notification Date	Response

After grants are received, prepare a similar chart to track interim reports (if required), final reports (if required), and thank you notes at the end of your project (whether required or not).

Mission Giving: Selected Additional Resources

Ashton, Debra. *The Complete Guide to Planned Giving*. Third edition. Debra Ashton, 2004.

Fredricks, Laura. *Developing Major Gifts*. Gaithersburg, MD: Aspen, 2001.

Panas, Jerold. *Asking*. Medfield, MA: Emerson and Church, 2002.

Stanley, Thomas J., and William D. Danko. *The Millionaire Next Door: The Surprising Secrets of America's Wealthy*. Marietta, GA: Longstreet Press, 1996.

www.ncpg.org (National Committee on Planned Giving)

Foundationcenter.org

Boardsource.org

Tgci.com (The Grantsmanship Center)

CHAPTER FOUR

STEWARDSHIP

If you haven't got any charity in your heart, you have the worst kind of heart trouble.

—Bob Hope

Thanks

Thank you. Thank you. Thank you. You just can't thank people enough.

But as my friend and colleague Diane Ward (whose company Membership Matters specializes in museum membership programs) regularly reminds her clients, "Show me that you know me." While a generic acknowledgment is better than nothing, how can your note to your member become more personalized? Isn't a new member a bit different from a returning member? Shouldn't someone who upgrades receive recognition for the increase?

Although it should not need to be said, I sometimes receive letters that are poorly printed, folded before the ink has dried so that the copy is smudged, and obviously mass produced. Just like your programs, the look and quality of your thank you note creates an impression of your museum. In your membership solicitation materials, you've likely told your prospects that they are special. That message of specialness begins with your first communication back to them, the acknowledgment.

75

Ideally, all thank you notes would be handwritten, but even in the smallest museum with a tiny giving program, that task will be overwhelming. But there are a few ways you can give the personal touch:

- If the letters are presigned in your word processing software, use blue ink for the signature. If you are able, set the margin for that blue signature a little to the left of the rest of your copy. This will help give the appearance of a hand-signed letter.

- When you enter the gift into your recordkeeping software, add a code for New, Renewal, Upgrade, Decrease. Then, as you print out your day or week of acknowledgment letters, create a report that lists all the names in that batch with their appropriate codes. If you hand-sign the letters (recommended), add a short handwritten note: "Thanks for the upgrade." "Thanks for renewing." If you know the member, handwrite more: "I can't wait to hear about your trip." "It was so good to see you at the last opening."

If your staff and your software are nimble, you can draft slightly different thank you letters. Letters to those who upgrade can mention the new benefits they will now receive. For example, "Thanks so much for upgrading to the Patron level. As a patron, you can enjoy our patrons-only lectures. In fact, the next patrons-only lecture on 'New Art from Guatemala' is set for March 19 at 7:00 p.m. I look forward to seeing you then so I can thank you in person."

The point of these letters is to encourage members to attend (and therefore become more likely to renew) and to build your personal relationship with them.

Giving and the Law

Like most other issues involving government, the legal requirements for museums and other nonprofit organizations around giving are a bit fuzzy. There are two mandates:

1. Donors of gifts of $250 or more must receive a written receipt. That's easy. As a good steward, the museum is going to acknowledge all gifts no matter what the size. As noted, such acknowl-

edgment provides an additional opportunity to inform the donor about the good work that the museum accomplishes because of generous gifts.

2. Donors of $75 or more must be notified if, in exchange for all or a portion of their gift, goods or services were received.

This second requirement is tricky. If your museum presents a fundraising concert, the fair market value of the tickets sold is not deductible. So for example, if world-class diva Miss Soprano sings on your behalf, you may look at what tickets for her performances cost at other venues, and then you can use that cost as a guide to deductibility. The key words are "fair market value." If you charge $100 per ticket, and tickets for Miss Soprano cost $50 elsewhere, then the fair market value is $50, and the remaining $50 is deductible.

How about a discount in your museum store at a certain level of membership? In this case, what you are offering is an "opportunity" to save money. That opportunity may or may not be used. At the time of signing up for membership, that opportunity cost does not reduce the tax-deductible portion.

Invitations to a private dinner? You must reduce the tax deductibility by the fair market value of the dinner. Even if every aspect of the dinner is donated by a caterer, that dinner still has a value.

One way around this thorny situation is to allow your higher-level members and donors the chance to opt out of benefits. This might make sense for mission-driven donors who live far away. But what about those people who live nearby? Do you really want them to not participate, to not attend, to not learn more about your work? I wouldn't promote this opt out opportunity. Let these donors motivated by tax savings come to you.

Discuss this issue of fair market value with your museum's accountant and lawyer, as well as with your development committee. Unfortunately, there are no clear answers, but at least you will not be the only one out on a limb.

Stewardship

Your current members and donors are your best prospects for higher levels of giving. Through your upper levels of membership and the annual fund,

SPECIAL STAKEHOLDER LETTER

Independence Seaport Museum

Philadelphia, Pennsylvania

Dear Friends,

In the late eighteenth century an epic American story began to unfold in Philadelphia, a story lasting centuries and involving hundred thousands of people. It would range across the oceans and involve nearly every nation that had an interest in the sea. It is a story we are all familiar with at some level, yet few of us seem to realize it started here, reached a pinnacle here, and continues to unfold here, albeit in a smaller way than in days past.

It is the story of the U.S. Navy.

Perhaps our story is overshadowed by the birth of the nation itself; the origins of the greatest sea power the world has ever seen might be small beans next to the origin story of the country that controls that power. Or maybe it is that none of the city's institutions have decided to pick this one up and trumpet it to the rest of the world, being preoccupied with other aspects of the city's profound impact on the rest of the country and the world. We have Independence Hall, the Liberty Bell, a Constitution Center, and soon will have a Museum of the American Revolution. It sometimes seems as though time stopped in this city with the ratification of the Constitution.

Of course time did not stop, nor did the impact of Philadelphia on the rest of the world. Not long after the basis of government was established, the need for assertiveness, and some muscle to back it up, became painfully obvious on the world stage. Our early merchants suffered piracy, impressment, and general disrespect. It soon became apparent that speedy ships alone would not suffice to keep trade alive. From the beginning, Philadelphia was the center of naval design, construction, and the manning of ships. The mythology and heroism that underpins a great naval tradition resides here. We mean to see that the city and the larger world come to recognize this.

Last year we completed an audience study and confirmed two things we had thought about our institution. The first is that we are a destination for tourists: 50 percent of our visitors are from out of town. The second is that those visitors want to see more naval history from us.

We have the resources to tell the story of the navy as no one else can. John Barry's papers are in our archives. There is a model by Joshua Humphries, designer of the first six frigates, including the *Constitution*, in one of our galleries. We have the personal effects of Stephen Decatur. We have the *Olympia* and the collections around her illustrating the age of steel and steam. We have the submarine USS

Becuna, representing the modern Navy of the early Cold War. In the coming year we will begin the task of arranging those resources in a way that tells a cohesive, sweeping, and great story. We will put the visitor on the deck of a sailing ship with Bainbridge and Barry. We will set sail across the Pacific with Dewey. We will prowl the depths with a submarine crew playing a deadly game of cat and mouse in the modern era. We will relate these stories to this city, the birthplace of the U.S. Navy and the U.S. Marine Corps.

These stories provide a framework for our historic ships to become more integrated with other objects and other programs. The stories also acknowledge all the engineers, inventors, and laborers who came here to work for the Navy, who stayed, and who helped our city grow.

Already, we have built deeper relationships with the Navy, with many of the new businesses that have opened at the Navy Yard, and with military history groups that have ties with Philadelphia. For example, many of our supporters had a chance to board the USS *Somerset* when it was docked outside our doors.

The naval history that began in colonial America continues now. With your continued enthusiasm, we will bring that essential history to our growing audience of tourists and Philadelphians.

Sincerely,

John Brady

President and CEO

Courtesy Independence Seaport Museum

---

people who have a high capacity to give have identified themselves. Some of these prospects may be at the top of their giving to you, but some can and will give more to the right project at the right time. That right time may be off into the future, so you need to take steps now to keep their interest alive. Some possibilities for stewarding these relationships include:

1. Schedule a coffee or lunch at least once a year with each of these prospects: no "ask," just updates and conversation about the future.

2. Invite them to dinner, cocktails, or dessert before or after an opening.

3. Invite them to join you at a school workshop.

4. Invite them to home parties.

5. Invite them to serve on a committee or on the board.

6. Have the board chairman meet one-on-one with all board members annually

7. Use an occasional special letter from the artistic directors for "insider" information.

8. Include handwritten notes on invitations.

9. Create a special, unexpected performance/or talk for an exclusive guest list.

10. Ask for their advice and/or use their expertise.

11. Send articles and stories of special interest: yours or theirs.

12. Send birthday cards, anniversary cards, or notes to honor other key life moments.

13. Ask them to play a volunteer role, chair a special effort, or host a dinner.

14. Ask them to introduce you to others.

Keep them informed of and engaged with the mission.

SURVIVAL

The life of a man consists not in seeing visions and in dreaming dreams, but in active charity and in willing service.

—Henry Wadsworth Longfellow

Putting It All Together

In brief, there is a lot going on. And many of the tasks, although leading toward different kinds of gifts, are going on simultaneously. Clearly, all this work won't happen by chance.

One way of making sense of all the activity is by creating a chart that focuses on each of your revenue goals. Such a chart helps you explain your work to other staff and to your board, providing a platform for your participation in budget conversations. A chart will also help to keep you focused. (Try meditation, too!) Each aspect of revenue is broken down into smaller goals. Table 5.1 is a revenue plan for a hypothetical museum.

Starting Your Development Plan

Once you have your goals established, you can start to flesh out your full plan with specific activities and costs. Table 5.2 is a sample of just the membership section.

Similar detail is needed for all the other aspects of your development program as noted on the revenue plan. After all of this is plotted, create a

Table 5.1.   Sample Annual Revenue Plan

INDIVIDUALS	#	$
Membership: General		
75% renewal of last year's 3,000 members @ $73 average	2,250	164,250
0.8% response to mail (35,000 pieces) @ $60 average	280	16,800
On-site sales	350	21,000
Web sales	200	12,000
Holiday gift membership sales	50	3,000
Board recruitment of new members	50	3,000
Upgrade campaign		1,500
TOTAL: GENERAL MEMBERSHIP (6% growth)	**3,180**	**221,550**
Membership: Leadership Club		
Leadership members: renewal @ $1,000	25	25,000
New leadership members @ $1,000	4	4,000
TOTAL: LEADERSHIP CLUB	**29**	**29,000**
Board Gifts		**22,000**
Annual Fund		
Renewals and upgrades		26,500
New gifts		3,000
TOTAL: ANNUAL FUND		**29,500**
INDIVIDUAL SPECIAL PROJECT GIFTS		**20,000**
FOUNDATIONS		
Anticipated renewal of program grants		35,000
New program grants (we have 6 prospects identified)		7,500
TOTAL: FOUNDATIONS		**42,500**
CORPORATIONS		
3 exhibitions sponsors @ $5,000		15,000
New initiative: business members 20 @ $100		2,000
TOTAL: CORPORATIONS		**17,000**
ANNUAL GALA		
Individual tickets @ $250	120	30,000
10 host tables of 8 @ $1,500	80	15,000
Major sponsor	16	10,000
Silent auction		25,000
TOTAL: GALA		**80,000**
PLANNED GIFTS		
Brochure conceived, designed, printed		
Start-up mailing list identified		
Small event for those known to have made planned gifts		
STEWARDSHIP		
TOTAL		**461,550**

Table 5.2. Development Budget Detail

INDIVIDUALS	#	$ GOAL	COST
Membership: General			
75% renewal of last year's 3,000 members @ $73 average	2,250	164,250	?
1. Monthly mailings of renewal packets			
2. Hand sign at X level and above			
3. Data entry on all renewals; reports to finance			
4. Acknowledgment letters and membership cards mailed to all renewals; hand sign at X level and above			
5. Second renewal notices to those who missed the first month			
6. Third renewal notices			
0.8% response to mail (35,000 pieces) @ $60 average	280	16,800	?
1. Packet content by DATE			
2. List selection by DATE			
3. Design by DATE			
4. Mailing coordinated with opening of major exhibition A			
5. PR support: Posters? Banners? More?			
6. New member acknowledgment letters drafted by DATE			
7. New member welcome gift			
8. New member event scheduled for 6 weeks into the run of major exhibition A: What? Who? Food? Music?			
On-site sales	350	21,000	?
1. Create special offer/materials by DATE			
2. Train visitor services staff			
Web sales	200	12,000	?
1. New copy written by DATE			
2. Special online offer?			
3. Who downloads and processes?			
Holiday gift membership sales	50	3,000	?
1. Conceive offer by DATE			
2. Write copy by DATE			
3. Design by DATE			
4. Hard mail or social media?			
Board recruitment of new members	50	3,000	?
1. Speak with CEO and board chair			
2. Special materials needed?			
Upgrade campaign		1,500	?
1. Conceive offer and lists			
2. Conceive special upgrade event			
3. Invitation copy by DATE			
4. Invitation design by DATE			
5. Mail by DATE			
Benefits fulfillment			
1. Plan membership opening events for each of the three major special exhibitions			
2. Invitations: copy, design, mail			
3. Patron level special event: plan, copy, design, mail			
4. Etc.			
Cultivation			
1. Identify and schedule three civic group talks			
2. Identify and schedule 3 home parties			
Programs			
1. Identify public programs where membership needs to have a presence: likelihood of largest crowds and new members joining			
TOTAL: GENERAL MEMBERSHIP (6% growth)	**3,180**	**221,550**	**?**

timeline of activities that need to be accomplished during each month. For example, in September, you might be

- completing copy for the direct mail piece (to be mailed early November).

- finalizing list selection for the direct mail packet.

- finalizing plans for the first membership opening event.

- mailing the first October renewal letters.

- mailing the second September renewal letters.

- Etc.

The finished timeline will start to look something like table 5.3.

Note how not all your activities will have immediate financial return. Be sure to include cultivation activities so that you are continually reaching out to new potential audiences.

Finally, you can use table 5.4 to keep your board and/or development committee informed of progress.

Continue in this manner for all the other areas of your development plan, giving you a way to compare progress against your plan and against last year. This structure also allows you to preempt some questions about discrepancies when the timing of an initiative this year may be different from last year.

Strategic Plan

We have talked a good deal about context: context in grant proposals, context in solicitations. What about context for you?

One of the most important of your development tools will be your strategic plan. Your plan will create the context for all of your asks. Because the planning process should involve many of your key people (staff and board) and because the plan should be formally adopted by the full board, the plan is a primary vehicle for keeping your most important efforts focused and energized. Here's what Lewis Carroll said in *Alice in Wonderland*:

"Would you tell me, please, which way I ought to go from here?"

Table 5.3. Sample Development Timeline

ACTIVITIES	Sept.	Oct.	Nov.	Dec.	Jan.	Feb.	Mar.	Apr.	May	June	July	Aug.
Draft end-of-year letter	x											
Design end-of-year letter		x										
Mail end-of-year letter			x									
Fall event invitation copy	x											
Fall event invitation design	x											
Etc.												
Etc.												

Table 5.4. Development Report November 20XX

Strategy	Last Year Goal $	Last Year at This Time $	This Year Goal $	Planned through Nov. 20XX $	Actual through Nov. 20XX $
Membership: General					
75% renewal of last year's 3,000 members @ $73 average			164,250		
0.8% response to mail (35,000 pieces) @ $60 average			16,800		
On-site sales			21,000		
Web sales			12,000		
Holiday gift membership sales			3,000		
Board recruitment of new members			3,000		
Upgrade campaign			1,500		
TOTAL: GENERAL MEMBERSHIP (6% growth)			221,550		
Etc.					
Etc.					
Etc.					

"That depends a good deal on where you want to get to," said the Cat.

"I don't much care where—" said Alice.

"Then it doesn't matter which way you go," said the Cat.

"—so long as I get SOMEWHERE," Alice added as an explanation.

"Oh, you're sure to do that," said the Cat, "if you only walk long enough."

If your museum wants to get things done, it surely does matter which way you go.

Your strategic plan is a tool primarily for internal use. It seems odd that a document that often includes strategies to address the competition would be posted on the museum's website. Keep it private, except for those who ask, such as foundations.

The planning process is sometimes precipitated by a major change in the museum's circumstances. For example, there is a change in leadership and a change in vision. Sometimes a plan results from a change in competition, such as the impending opening of a new museum nearby. Or the plan might begin when the museum discovers that it is lost, simply drifting from one activity to the next. The best museums plan on a regular cycle, with a new plan developed every three or four years.

The strategic plan identifies direction and priorities, allowing the most useful choices to be made. Everyone gets on the same page so that we know that this set of actions is most important, while this other set of actions needs to take a back seat for a bit. The plan helps to align the work of all the departments, all the volunteers. We are going to talk about this; we are not going to emphasize that.

The components of the strategic plan are:

1. History: A brief history to help explain how we got to now.

2. Mission: Why does the organization exist? This should be a short statement, two sentences at most. In the past, many museums had language that was object focused, variations on the words, "Get. Keep. Show. Tell." But I suggest changing the direction of the mission by starting with the people served. For example, "Our Town Museum educates children and adults in this region by. . . ." As noted earlier, the objects will never know if the mission is helping or not. People will know.

3. <u>Vision</u>: What does the organization want to achieve at the end of a certain period of time? How will it be different? In three years or five years? Very often this expression of the vision begins at the staff (programmatic) level, then the full planning team is brought in to buy into the vision. This is where I typically spend a lot of time. It describes where we're going. Museum directors sometimes are reluctant to be pinned down by a concrete statement, but without such language how can others shape their work?

4. <u>Competition</u>: Among other organizations, what is the organization's competitive advantage? For some small museums, competition may include large museums. For other small museums, competition may be high school football. What are the dynamics for you? What can you offer that no one else can offer?

5. <u>Values or guiding principles</u>: How we are going to work. For example, "Everything we do for the public will be: Experiential, Interdisciplinary, Experimental." Sometimes this is helpful, sometimes not. Statements like "We will be excellent" are cliché and meaningless.

6. <u>Self-Analysis/SWOT</u>: Strengths. Weaknesses. Opportunities. Threats.

    a. What strengths does the organization have that will help it achieve the vision?

    b. What weaknesses does the organization have that will prevent it from achieving the vision?

    c. What factors outside the organization will help it achieve the vision?

    d. What factors outside the organization will get in the way of achieving the vision?

7. <u>Strategies</u>: What are three to five strategies that you just have to do if the vision is to be achieved? These are large overarching statements about how you're going to get to your vision given your strengths, weaknesses, opportunities, and challenges. Some sample ideas include:

- We will make our setting our competitive advantage.

- We will set a new standard for the visitor experience.

- We will change our name to better reflect what we do.

- We will demonstrate our increasing value to the region.

8. Goals: In each of the major areas of the organization what are one or two measurable goals?

   Sample major areas include:

   Program (often subsets of this)

   - By 20XX, augment the visual arts experience with an ongoing schedule of performances, events, and programs that attract a broad array of new audiences and that generate earned income.

   - By 20XX, increase earned income from our shop by $XXX through an aggressive program of sales and customer service.

   Staff

   - By 20XX, we will add a science educator to the staff to create school programs aligned with state objectives.

   Board

   - By 20XX, we will add four new board members from beyond our core three-county region.

   Facility

   Funds

   Marketing

   Development

   Administration

9. Tasks: Break down each task into specific actions: Who is accountable, on what timetable? Does this impact the budget? For example, what tasks might be necessary in order to meet the

board objective? Who is going to do them? When? Those tasks might include:

- Nominating committee appoints an expansion task force.

- Expansion task force identifies key community leaders in the areas immediately outside our core region.

- Task force meets with those leaders and seeks recommendations.

- For each recommendation, a series of informational, education, and cultivation steps is planned and initiated.

- Etc.

Among the many tasks is a specific assignment for the board chair to monitor how we are doing against the plan.

10. <u>Multiyear (three-year) budget</u>: It is very hard to project beyond a few years.

End of strategic plan.

Such a plan provides a ton of ammunition for the development staff. It provides direction and context for grant proposals. It helps set goals. (If we are going to do X in three years, we will need more money.) It provides common language for conversations with other staff and with the board. It addresses operational needs within the development area as well as for the whole museum. Portions of the plan can be "leaked" to key donors to help them get excited.

Roles and Responsibilities

A phrase that has become popular, especially in job descriptions, is "create a culture of philanthropy." Yes, the head of development has a key part to play in informing others and engaging others in achieving the museum's goals. This task, however, is doomed unless all the top people begin with an understanding of their roles and responsibilities. In some museums, especially smaller museums that might be hiring a first chief development officer (CDO), there is an inclination by the CEO and/or board chair to assume that once the chief development officer position is filled, everything involving fundraising is now off their plates. Nothing could be farther from the truth. A well-functioning culture of philanthropy looks something like this:

Chief Development Officer (who may be the director and/or chief marketing officer, too)

- Recommends and monitors the overall development strategy

- Recommends and secures director and board approval of development goals for each area of activity, including identification, information, cultivation, solicitation, and stewardship

- Educates and engages staff (all of them), the board, and other volunteers in the implementation of the development plan

- Creates key philanthropic messages and materials

- Creates systems for recording, tracking, and analyzing gifts and relationships

- Secures board approval for policies and procedures

- Regularly reports to the board (and committees) on progress

- Identifies prospects, cultivates relationships, solicits gifts when she or he is the best "fit," stewards relationships

- Serves on the senior management team and helps to frame the strategic direction of the museum

- Represents the museum to various constituencies

- Donates at a pace-setting level for other staff

Director

- Includes development objectives in the consideration of exhibition and program plans

- Approves the development plan and helps present and promote it to the board

- Works with the CDO to create a personal target list of activities for identifying, educating, cultivating, soliciting, and stewarding key institutional relationships

- Encourages other staff to participate in various aspects of the development plan

- Represents the museum

- Donates at a pace-setting level

Board

- Each board member gives at a pace-setting level

- Approves the development plan

- Participates in achieving the goals of the development plan; each board member has a set of development goals

- Attends events and programs and helps to greet, host, meet, and thank prospects

- Keeps development staff informed about prospects

- Represents the museum to various constituencies

Other Staff

- Presents outstanding experiences every day

- Understands that excellent customer service is essential

- Helps build relationships and keeps development staff informed

- Participates in various aspects of the development plan, with some staff joining key meetings with prospects

- Provides information and budgets for grants

- Represents the museum to various constituencies

Fear of Trying

You can almost feel the wave of panic sweep over the room.

So often when I'm asked to speak to boards about their fundraising responsibilities, I can predict the faces turning down or away, arms folding over chests, sighing, and moaning. Invariably, many of the people in the room have never before asked for money, but they have a sense that this will be a task ranging from perhaps difficult to repugnant.

Here are two ways of getting that conversation started:

1. Ask each person in the room to speak about what attracted him/ her to that particular organization, and what is the organization's best work. After allowing a few minutes for quiet reflection, ask some or all in the group to talk about their answers. What happens from this sharing is a glow of good feeling that comes from shifting the focus away from money and toward the work. The board members discover that it is easy—maybe even pleasant—to talk about outstanding programs with impact. This ease of conversation, they will learn, is 80 percent of asking for a gift. After all, it is not really about dollars; money is merely the tool that allows good work to happen. Do we want to experience more good work? If yes, then we must do what we have to do.

2. a. Ask each person in the room to think about a donation made to another organization. "Think about how you were asked for that donation. Was it by mail? In person? Think about how the gift was made. Did you sit down and write a check? Did you respond online? Think about how you felt making that gift."

   b. Now don't talk about the gift; talk about your feelings when you were making those gifts. Most people will say that it felt good, that they felt proud, glad to help, knew that they were doing some good. Sometimes I'll hear how someone was continuing a tradition started in an earlier generation, or how a particular organization helped in a time of need. For most people, making a donation feels good. (Okay, to be honest, in one group, one person said that he resented having his arm twisted by someone who, at a later date, was surely going to be asked for a gift in return.) But by and large, giving is a positive experience. When we ask someone to help our favorite cause with a charitable gift, we are providing a reason to feel good. A conversation about money is not painful for the person being asked.

With these two conversations as backdrop, the stage is set for a discussion on when and how to ask. The wave of panic has abated. The board is ready.

CHAPTER FIVE

Your Best Friends

A development director's best friends may not sit on the development committee. The people who can help the most may be sitting somewhere else.

Recently, I was asked to serve on a nonprofit board in the Philadelphia region. As part of that ask (as nice as the email was, it should have been in person), I was told that "there won't be too many meetings, and you don't have to give very much." These combined disclaimers on my future obligation were the kiss of death. Why would I want to serve on a board that doesn't take its responsibilities seriously?

The people most able to assure your future development success are currently serving on your nominating committee. Who are they enlisting to be the next leaders of your organization? The width of the circle of influence of incoming trustees is as important as the depth of their pockets. Have they been enlisted with a clear understanding of their fundraising responsibilities? Are they willing to approach others? If they say "no" to fundraising during the recruitment phase, how likely will they be to help the cause later on?

At the very least, the head of development should help inform the nominating process. In the strongest organizations, the development director is a full voting member of the nominating committee.

The other key group of development friends sits on the finance committee. While it is easy to plug in numbers ("We'll raise 10 percent more next year"), the head of development should insist on submitting a fully explored development plan. First, review this detailed plan with your CEO and be sure to have her or his full support. Share the plan with the development committee so that they (not you) can recommend the plan to finance. Then share the path to the numbers with the numbers people. Show how much, based on your history, is likely to come via mail renewal, how much is likely to require personal follow up, how much is likely to be lost, and what is the plan to make up for lost gifts and secure new ones.

In this plan, include where board help will be needed. "In order to achieve ten new major gifts, we are counting on thirty new leads from the board and twenty-five new solicitations by board members." "We will need five board members to host home events as a recruitment tool." "We will need two board members to help with follow-up calls to past donors." Break your year down into tiny pieces. Be specific. And be specific about what goals will not be reached if there is less than the required help from the board. "Okay, in that case, we're likely to raise several thousand dollars less, meaning we'll have to reduce our mission-related program. I see no other way." (Be sure that you really do not see another way.) Be prepared for pushback suggesting higher direct mail rates, higher onsite sales, higher whatever. But at some point, the numbers do not add up unless the board pitches in, taking on the very responsibility they knew about when they were recruited by the nominating committee.

Is this planning a lot of work? Yes, but it is less work—and better for your sleep—than scrambling at the end of the year to hit the targets.

The head of development should not be expected to create miracles. But it is fair to expect a detailed and well-executed plan in which the full team of staff members and board is deeply engaged.

THE CAPITAL CAMPAIGN

Find out how much God has given you and from it take what you need; the remainder is needed by others.

—Saint Augustine

Capital Campaign: Before You Begin to Begin

Your museum's capital assets include the building(s) and contents, your collections, and your reserve funds and/or endowment. A capital campaign is an organized effort to increase all or some part of those assets. It may be that you are just focused on the building, perhaps an expansion or a major rehabilitation of your spaces, or it may be that your campaign includes elements of construction plus significant additions to the collection funds plus growth of your endowment.

Unfortunately, sometimes there are circumstances that force a capital campaign without much planning: a tornado or a flood destroys parts of your museum. The best situation, however, is one in which the campaign results from careful and thoughtful planning. That planning often begins with a new strategic plan in which the director, the board, and the staff participate in the creation of a new vision for the museum. Perhaps the recent acquisition of an enormous and noteworthy collection requires new space. Maybe years of "just getting by" have resulted in a long list of necessary building repairs and systems upgrades. Or public demand and participation has increased to the point that small classrooms can no longer handle the crowd, that the old elevator cannot move the numbers of people showing up for the blockbuster exhibit, or that quaint lobby from days gone by has no room for visitors and their coats or for a ticketing station, a coat room, and a museum store. Possibly your director and board are convinced that a few more major objects on view will tantalize new visitors to come and enjoy.

In these situations, the new vision for the future often means a long list of changes and improvements. Is the vision, that core idea that will be at the heart of your campaign, compelling? To be successful, what you need most is an idea that captures the imagination of your prospects. You're not just raising money. You are helping them fulfill their dreams for your museum and for your community/audience. Sometimes your planning team may need to add to the first list of needs. Yes, your museum may need new plumbing and new HVAC, but will those needs ignite excitement among your prospects? Even though the dollar goal may go up, you may want to add more sizzle to your list of improvements so that the whole project is easier to sell.

Sometimes one thing leads to another. "If we move the elevator to the front lobby, then we also need to move. . . ." How will these improvements be made? What will they cost? What additional operating costs are implied? "If we add three more classrooms to meet demand, do we need more educators on staff?" Does your museum "family" have the necessary talent to implement the changes, or will you need to bring in outside advisors, contractors, designers, etc.?

This early financial planning phase is critical to your campaign success. Surely you don't want to discover huge new expenses after you've announced a campaign goal. Be sure that your planned expenses are comprehensive, with line items for the capital campaign itself, for any benefits (such as recognition signage that may be offered), and for additional public relations around the reopening, etc. In addition, this early planning provides a wonderful opportunity to build ownership of the campaign. Bring campaign thoughts through all of your committees. What are the collections implications? What are the financial implications? What will happen to the public experience during construction, and what will that mean for annual projections of attendance, membership, shop sales, etc.? Because ultimately, every aspect of the museum may be impacted, and surely the changes will be exciting, now is a good time to bring more key people into board or committee roles. If yours is a museum that receives municipal or county funding, have an early conversation with those essential government leaders: "This is what we're thinking."

Only when all this early planning is complete and you have a good sense of the focus and scale of a campaign may you begin to think about language that helps you summarize the effort. Some language, like "Campaign for Excellence," is so overused no one will hear it. What few words will help you sell the big idea to your public? The idea of "your public" is key. The language that works elsewhere may not work for you.

Capital Campaign: Before You Begin/Feasibility

You've done your homework. You have a detailed and comprehensive budget and your staff and board are chomping at the bit.

Not so fast.

Just because the "family" is excited, will others be enthusiastic to the point of opening their wallets, checkbooks, and bank accounts? Is the idea really that wonderful? Are the people who could make or break your campaign ready to give at the levels you imagine? Are there other key people you haven't considered as donors or as campaign leaders?

Before jumping in too deep, after the early planning, most museums take a short breather to conduct a feasibility study. Before the full resources of the board and staff are committed to raising large dollars, it makes sense to check that the case for support resonates with potential contributors and that donors capable of giving large gifts are willing to give at or near the high amounts you imagine.

For some organizations, the campaign feasibility study, at least in the old definition, no longer makes sense. In more sophisticated settings, people with giving capacity and influence already have been brought onto the board or into other key volunteer roles, and they have been part of the early decision making about how to address institutional needs. By the time the "Do we do a campaign?" question is asked, the answer from these leaders already should be known. There's no need for a big study to confirm what has been decided. For these organizations, it is not a question of "Do we move forward?" but rather "How? And When?" What if the richest person in town, someone who certainly has the capacity to give you $1 million, has just made a major commitment to a college elsewhere and is prepared to give your campaign a gift of only $10,000 per year? What if while you have been planning, the regional symphony orchestra has been quietly planning as well? What would simultaneous campaigns mean for your donors and for the potential of your success?

In some other organizations, much of capital funding is likely to come from foundation and/or government sources that either will not agree to an hour of their time to answer feasibility questions or cannot predict or won't reveal a year ahead of time how a proposal will fit into a funding cycle.

So should your museum conduct a campaign feasibility study? Yes.

In addition to the traditional questions about moving ahead with a campaign or not, think about the feasibility study addressing other kinds of questions. Use the museum's focus on the future to:

- Engage civic and community leaders. Make sure those influencers are supportive of your mission, your programs, and your needs. Test out your message. The language that is effective in a study will likely be effective in a proposal later.

- Reach out to people who have not been involved. Seek out some nay-sayers and ask their opinions. It is likely that their negative opinions are shared by others, and those opinions are often based on ignorance. Use the study to educate and to determine how to correct misconceptions about who you are and what you do.

- Reveal new prospects. Ask your strongest supporters about who else should be involved and about why those prospects are not currently engaged. The first step for these new prospects may not be the capital campaign, but possibly you can use the excitement of expansion or construction to involve prospects in new cultivation opportunities.

In short, your capital campaign is part of your long-term integrated development program. In addition to helping you reach your campaign goals, think about how a feasibility study can advance your efforts to identify new prospects, to inform them, and to involve them.

The study typically involves a number of interviews with the key people your museum has identified. The study group should include some of your highest capacity prospects, some civic champions (who may be knowledgeable of competing campaigns), some political and/or business leaders, some rising stars who might be future leaders of your museum, one or two influencers who have not been involved with your museum, etc. The study group may be as many as thirty people (but because a few people may say "No" to the study, start with a larger group of names).

The study group is more likely to be open and honest with someone who is neutral. So most feasibility studies are conducted by outside consultants who promise interviewees that conversations will be confidential. Interview several consultant candidates so that you understand the nuances of different interview techniques. When you have made a choice, the consultant will meet with you, learn about your museum, discuss the group to be interviewed, and then take over with scheduling and meeting. You may receive an interim report partway through the study. At the end of the study, you should receive a written report with recommendations on how to proceed.

Of course, each consultant has an individualized approach to conducting a study, but the interviews likely will touch on at least these issues:

- What are overall perceptions of the museum?

- How are the staff and board leadership perceived? Is there a sense that the board and staff have the capacity to execute the campaign?

- What programs resonate the most?

- What aspects of the museum are considered strengths and weaknesses?

- Is the case exciting and motivating?

- Do constituents feel that the campaign goal can be met?

- Do interviewees know of key people who should be approached for dollars and/or to play leadership roles in the campaign?

- Are there any factors that might get in the way of campaign success?

This process will take several months, time well spent if it leads you to new pockets of support while it helps you avoid mines in the field. Bring the final feasibility report back to your planning group for deep discussion. That conversation will be the blueprint for your campaign.

Capital Campaign: Almost Ready

Annual support must come first. What good is the new building or the new wing if the museum lacks the funds to operate it? If a prospect asks if you prefer continuation of a gift to the annual fund or a substitute gift to the capital campaign, choose the annual fund.

Many prospects, however, will be in a position to help in every possible way. These people will already be members and will already give to the annual fund. Rather than annoying them by going back to them for one thing after the other, approach these prospects for a "comprehensive gift," one that includes continuation of their membership and annual fund gifts, plus a new commitment to the capital project. "Betty and John, we would like you to consider a comprehensive gift of $1,500 a year for three years. Each year, we will allocate $400 to continue your membership at your current level, and $100 per year will sustain your annual fund gift. $1,000 times three or $3,000 will count toward the capital campaign, making you eligible for recognition on permanent signage in the lobby." Yes, this creates a minor (but happy) bookkeeping problem, but surely Betty and John will have an easier time thinking this way about their finances rather than worrying what may happen when you come back again.

Although your nominating committee may have diligently prepared each of your board members for potential roles as solicitors, some people simply hate asking for money. Why put someone into an uncomfortable position in which failure is likely? Find something else for that board member to do.

Some members of your board may have been involved with a capital campaign for their college or university, or perhaps they helped on a campaign for a much larger institution. If so, they may anticipate a sophisticated campaign structure with an executive committee and subcommittees focused on businesses or major donors or some other group of prospects. In a smaller museum, it will be unlikely that you have enough capable volunteers to fill all those committee roles. Ultimately, even in some large organization campaigns, the majority (if not all) of the solicitations are completed by a handful of people. Instead of spending weeks or months trying to fill a large number of subcommittee spots, get the most powerful and eager group of ten or twelve people onto your one and only campaign committee. Then if you need help from others ("Sam, we know that you do business with the XYZ Company. Can you help us get in the door?"), ask for it on a very limited and specific basis. If you need them, you can add more volunteers later, but nothing is more of a drag than a group of volunteers who won't show for meetings, or worse, need updates on everything when they occasionally do appear.

An exception to this suggestion of fewer committees comes with campaigns for new construction. Unless you have a construction project manager on staff, you will be helped by a building committee who can review and approve project plans, argue over overspending, and keep an eye on the timeline.

In some campaigns, it is helpful to create an honorary committee filled with all those government, civic, and philanthropic names that will assure the public that the "right" people are behind the effort.

Before you start asking for money, your campaign committee has a few practical issues to address:

1. What will be the payout period of the campaign? Will prospects have three years to fulfill their pledges? Five years? How does this payout period relate to when you need the money? If construction starts before all the money comes in, will you need a bridge loan so that the contractors can be paid? Will that loan have a cost? If so, you must add the cost to your campaign budget.

2. What kinds of gifts will you accept? Cash and checks are easy. What about stock? If someone wants to make a gift of highly appreciated stock, does the museum have procedures in place to redeem it? How and when will the gift be valued?

3. Will the museum accept gifts of objects or real estate given with the donor's understanding that these gifts will be sold? Do you want to be, or are you prepared to be, in the sales or real estate business?

4. Corporate matching gifts toward the campaign should be treated just like they are treated elsewhere: they count toward the individual donor's total.

5. Will your museum offer naming opportunities? At what levels and for what spaces/programs/positions? Increasingly, arts organizations are finding that less is more, that audiences are bothered by acknowledgment signs on every closet and every window. The new wing or the new gallery are good choices. The new classroom or the new lobby, good. But at some level (perhaps $5,000 or $10,000), the donor acknowledgment is a name listed among another names on a beautiful and creative wall sign. If you are planning new construction, you are probably spending a sizeable sum on design. Don't let little plaques get in the way.

Simultaneously, for very large gifts, donors may name a position, likely starting from a pool of those several most prestigious positions in the museum: director, curators, chief educator.

6. Note that these naming opportunities are not aligned with actual costs. As an outcome of your successful campaign, you may just be painting your Impressionist Gallery while you are building a brand new space to exhibit Obscure Ancient Artists. The Impressionist Gallery will most likely be more interesting to more donors, so the price for naming that space should be higher. This naming task is about value rather than cost.

Your planning committee should decide on all these details. Through the details, they will "own" the campaign.

Campaign Tools

Prospect list. Many of these names will be people you know well. Others may be donors to other efforts in your region and/or in your discipline. Some may require extensive research, while others will be well documented.

Gift table. This is a chart that suggests how many gifts you will need at each level in order to reach your goal. For example, for a $2 million campaign, you might be seeking what is shown in table 6.1.

Of course, there are other formulas that could be more suited to your donors and the standards of giving in your region. Start with the largest gift you imagine you will receive and then work down through the various levels using your knowledge of your donor base. It is easy enough to list so many

Table 6.1.   Capital Campaign Gift Table

		TOTAL
1 gift @	$250,000	$250,000
3 gifts @	$100,000	$300,000
5 gifts @	$75,000	$225,000
8 gifts @	$50,000	$400,000
16 gifts @	$25,000	$400,000
25 gifts @	$10,000	$250,000
50 gifts @	$5,000	$50,000
100 gifts @	$1,000	$100,000
Misc. gifts		$25,000
		$2,000,000

gifts at a particular level, but are there real prospects for these gifts? As you are creating the table, pencil in the names of likely prospects.

One point made by this table is that just a few gifts at the top make or break the campaign. A second point is that ultimately the campaign will need several hundred donors. Because some prospects will not give and because some prospects will give below your carefully researched amount, your campaign will need more than several hundred prospects. Some campaigns have used this chart in their materials to help prospects understand the high levels of giving required.

Case Statement. Often this is the campaign booklet, beautifully designed and written with compelling and emotional language. Use the best of the language you developed for your feasibility study. What words and images are important for your constituencies? What design elements will help prospects look at every page? What do you want prospects to feel as they peruse the booklet? What can your campaign literature say about the museum that will be made possible by a successful campaign? Remember, you don't need money; you need what money can buy.

Pledge Form. Be sure to include a place for donors to indicate matching gifts. And why not ask now how they want their names listed? This saves a step later.

Return Envelope. For the pledge form.

Naming Opportunities. If you are providing them, be sure that they correspond to your gift table.

Cover Letter. Optional. Most, if not all, of your early conversations will happen in person. Instead of a cover letter, for those prospects who need a little time to decide, send a letter after the solicitation meeting.

In case the prospect misplaces part of the packet, be sure to have your museum's name, address, and phone number on every piece.

The Quiet Campaign

It is impossible to know in advance all of the factors that may influence the outcome of a capital campaign. Many of those factors are out of the control of you and your colleagues. What if the largest company in your region decides to move its facility to another state? What if the nearby military base closes? What if the leading philanthropist in your community suddenly remarries and sails off in his yacht, never to be seen again? Although you have done everything well so far, you have a long way to go.

Most campaigns begin with a "quiet campaign," a focus on those select prospects who are most likely to make the largest gifts. There are a few reasons for starting this way:

- What if most of those largest gifts do not materialize? What are the chances for success if you are depending on many, many small contributions? Surely the odds turn against success. Rather than risk an enormous public embarrassment for you and your team, pursue those big gifts that get you most of the way. Some consultants will suggest 70 percent, 80 percent, or more of the total should be committed before you go public.

- Your early prospects will be flattered that they are being brought into the discussion before the hoi polloi. Some of these prospects/donors will even suggest others with significant means who should be involved.

- These early donors help set a standard of giving for others. If Person A is perceived as making a "stretch gift" (something beyond his or her ordinary), others may be inspired to make a "stretch gift," too.

- These quiet conversations continue to provide important feedback that can be used to adjust your message.

This quiet phase can go on for quite a few months, maybe even a year or more. This surely will be the longest part of your total effort. The key to success is careful matching of solicitors with prospects. Who knows the prospect best? Who will have the most influence? Each high-level prospect name should be discussed by your team so that the best solicitor comes to light. That solicitor may be a volunteer on the team, the director, the chief development officer (perhaps that is the director, too), or someone else from the community entrusted with this important task.

Ideally, the solicitor is assisted by whatever background research can be provided as well as a strategy for the conversation. However, it is likely that at least some of the prospects at these highest levels, and their circumstances, will be well known, so you may be able to just begin.

As in other kinds of asking, the words "Join me" are powerful. It will help the solicitors if they are among the earliest donors to the campaign. It helps further if they can demonstrate their stretch. Some people will say they should make a "sacrificial gift," a surprisingly strong statement about their support. Some people will say, "Give until it hurts." Others will say, "Go deeper than the hurt, and give until it feels good."

We must be mindful again about donor motivation. Some prospects will want to see their names on the wall. Some will want to be honored some other way. Some will give anonymously. Know your prospects. What makes them tick?

This is work! The tasks include research, engaging solicitors, keeping everyone on task, and following up with acknowledgment letters and other materials. One of the questions you addressed in the feasibility study is whether or not your museum has the staff capacity to manage this work. Most museums retain a consultant to help.

The consultant's assignments may include some or all these needs: prospect research, scheduling meetings and preparing agendas, creating strategies for some or all of the prospects, writing and designing materials, keeping records of gifts in progress and gifts received, etc. In addition, the consultant can provide an objective view of your challenges and your progress. Of course, the more the consultant is asked to do, the higher the bill will be, but this may be the only way the work can get done. The cost of not having outside help may be a campaign that never picks up full speed. If you choose to use a consultant, the expense should be added to your campaign total.

The Public Campaign

Some campaigns reach their goals or close to it before "going public." The initial group of donors, those closest to the museum, are generous beyond anyone's wildest imaginings, and the money has flowed in. Best of all, gifts have required relatively little expense. The next phase, usually involving reaching out to hundreds or thousands of households, quickly becomes a logistical and a financial challenge.

Why go public?

On the TV show *Roseanne* (1988–1997), when the mother (comedian Roseanne Barr) wanted to punish her kids, she threatened them with a trip to the museum. The TV audience laughed. It is probable that many people in your market area have a preconception of your museum as a stuffy "old boys club," snooty, boring, not for them. Now, when there is a special excitement in the museum because of the campaign, is a perfect time to start tearing down barriers to participation. "If you think it's not for you, think again." "If you think it is just for the wealthiest few, come to a Sunday afternoon family program." "Did you know that we have an extensive after-school program, that we reach out to seniors, that we work on curriculum with teachers, that we receive critical acclaim, that we attract thousands of tourists, that we add significantly to the local economy, etc.?" Rather than risk having people in your community criticize the museum for not even asking, use the campaign to invite everyone in and to give everyone a chance to participate. Especially if yours is a museum that receives local government funding, even if someone gives just a dollar, that gift represents a vote for you, a bond with your future.

Sending your campaign message to large numbers has costs. Most capital campaigns use some sort of direct mail packet (outer envelope, cover letter, brochure, response/pledge card, reply envelope). Use the packet to show off. Use the best photography. If appropriate, show families, show people of various ages and backgrounds, mention your best programs. You may need to acquire mailing lists, or you may be able to exchange lists from other nonprofit organizations. Time your mailing with an announcement through the media. Follow up with more media stories, interviews, and profiles. This is the time to be best buddies with whoever handles museum PR. Social media is helpful too. You can augment all of this outreach with lobby displays, posters at local businesses, signs in otherwise vacant storefronts, etc. Show that you are a "player" in your community.

This public phase also provides a wonderful opportunity to reach out to organized groups. Consider a round of speaking engagements at local service organizations as well as at private home gatherings. Some people will want to play a role now. For others, you are planting the seeds for future involvement.

During this public phase, all of your other development work continues. You still promote membership. (Especially if your campaign will lead to new construction, people will want to have the chance to see it first.) You still manage your annual fund and your major gifts.

Sometimes, because of the enormous excitement about the future, there is pressure to have a groundbreaking or other ceremony before the campaign is over. Try to hold off. It is much more difficult to raise money when there is a hole in the ground. Potential donors will run for the hills if they think their dollars are not needed.

A strategy used at this time by many museums is a challenge or match campaign. In a challenge, a donor promises to give a large—perhaps the final—gift if some amount of other dollars can be raised in a specified amount of time. In a match, a donor promises to give an additional dollar (or two!) for every dollar raised in a certain amount of time. Either strategy can help motivate prospects to take action sooner rather than later. It is not unusual for that challenge or match to come from a gift that already has been "secretly" pledged.

This portion of the campaign is about hoopla. Keeping the museum on the public's radar for a long period time requires high energy, high staff and volunteer commitment, and high funds. The return on this investment will be dollars toward your campaign and new enthusiasm for the museum when the successful campaign is concluded.

Surprise: The End Is Just the Beginning

"All my life's a circle, sunrise and sundown." In his song "All My Life's a Circle," the songwriter Harry Chapin must have had some experience as a museum development professional. Surely the receipt of that gift that brings your museum over the capital campaign goal is a time for celebration. The pressure is off, and the museum can proceed on its plans with confidence. It also is a time to reexamine the entire development program. During the campaign, the relationship your donors have with the museum has deepened; they have invested in your future. Some have given at levels beyond anything they have given before, revealing new interest and revealing capacity. Many, many people are proud. The next development cycle has begun.

Start with the joy:

1. A moment of tempering: Speak with your director and the campaign chair. Are there many prospects still in play? Is there the potential for many more gifts to come in the near future? Are you awaiting final word on a huge grant? It may make sense to keep a lid on the enthusiasm for a little while so that you have received just about everything.

2. Once you decide that *it is time*, be sure to notify your committees, your board, and any other staff and volunteers who have helped reach the goal. Ask them to hold back on sharing the news with others. Most won't wait.

3. Draft a media release. Simultaneously, plan a media event followed immediately by a victory celebration. Be sure to honor your chairman and your volunteers.

4. Schedule an additional event to thank the staff.

5. Write thank you notes to chairs, volunteers, and staff.

6. Draft final invoices and thank you notes for gifts.

   a. Prepare language for recognition signage (if appropriate for your campaign).

   b. Celebrate with the public.

      • Victory signage in the museum

      • If relevant, a sequence of opening events

   c. Use your success to build new awareness.

   d. Take a vacation.

   e. Speak with your most generous donors. Ask them if they are aware of new prospects who have surfaced because of the campaign.

   f. Be sure to inform foundations of your success. Include information in your next proposals.

   g. As donors complete their pledges, assess their interest and capacity to give at higher than their previous levels to the annual fund.

   h. Start a higher level of donors within your major gifts group.

Then, with other staff, start to address the question of "Now what?" Many of the staff may feel let down. After a long period of intense activity, they may feel they have little to do. Help them and yourself start to think about the future. Start to dream again.

Capital Campaigns: Selected Additional Resources

Dove, Kent E. *Conducting a Successful Capital Campaign.* San Francisco: Jossey-Bass, 1988.

Lysakowski, Linda, and Judith Snyder. *Getting Ready for a Capital Campaign: Your Blueprint for Evaluating Internal and External Readiness.* Alexandria, VA: Association of Fundraising Professionals, 2002.

Walker, Julia Ingraham. *Nonprofit Essentials: The Capital Campaign.* Hoboken, NJ: Wiley, 2005.

CHAPTER SEVEN
A DEVELOPMENT WRITING TOOLKIT

Be the change you want to see in the world.

—Mahatma Gandhi

Make These Ideas Your Own

What skills are needed to be an effective head of development? I think the list is short. In such a people-centered profession, most important is the skill of listening. More essential than your ability to manipulate metrics or to hire a wonderful caterer for your next event is your ability to listen to your various constituents. What are your visitors saying in the galleries or as they leave your museum? What do civic influencers say about the role of the museum in the community? What is behind the donor's rejection of your current appeal? I'm not sure this skill can be taught by anything other than practice.

Likewise, the person responsible for development must be a good observer. You must watch body language, watch who talks with whom, observe what objects visitors skip in the galleries, and see who is standing alone.

At "Career Days," when students have asked me what skills are required for this field, I usually get a laugh when I mention juggling. The development director must juggle multiple tasks, multiple projects at one time, and many, many relationships.

And then, because so much development work is about communication, facility with words is key. One must be an articulate speaker, and one must be a good writer. Written materials run the gamut from brief thank you notes to lengthy capital campaign materials. Even if some of this work

113

is accomplished by other staff or by consultants, the development director must check for accuracy and tone. Are the messages correct? Is the language consistent with other marketing and development messaging?

Some writing examples appear earlier in this book. The following grouping of samples is intended to focus on the thought process. Obviously, some of the language is specific to a particular museum or a specific situation. Please find a way to adapt the language to your organization, to your community, and to the tone you need for you and for the uniformity among all your communications that is part of your "brand."

The first examples relate to renewals of membership and the annual fund. The tone is very light, certainly not scolding. There's no red stamp saying "SECOND NOTICE" or worse, "FINAL NOTICE." The member or donor is part of your family. The assumption is that the lapse of response is simply an oversight. (When I've used these ideas, some members and donors wrote apology notes, "So sorry I forgot. Of course, I want to renew!" Clearly, these folks got the message that they were more than just a number.)

With just a few changes, the annual fund phone script could be used for membership renewal as well. I also give you a sample Tributes form.

SAMPLE FORM 7.1

SAMPLE MEMBERSHIP RENEWAL REMINDER

Dear Friend:

Hocus pocus.

With three young children at home, things are always disappearing in my house. Maybe that happens at your house too.

We recently sent a membership renewal notice to your home. Did it disappear? I hope you're planning to renew your membership so you'll continue to enjoy the benefits of the Museum of Our Town.

Please send in your renewal today. Our wonderful year of special programs and exhibitions will not happen by magic. We are counting on the interest and generosity of good friends like you.

Thanks.

Sincerely,

XXX

September 2014

XXX
XXX
XXX

Dear XXX,

Is your desk like mine? As much as I promise myself to keep things neat, the task of straightening up keeps getting away from me. Items that need some attention somehow slip to the bottom.

Perhaps that happens to you too.

We recently sent you a notice about renewing your annual fund commitment to the James A. Michener Art Museum. If despite your best efforts that notice somehow slipped to the bottom, here is a <u>friendly reminder</u>.

Contributions to the annual fund transform our building into a thriving regional art center. For more than twenty-five years, through gifts to the annual fund, the Michener has been able to sustain its many exhibitions and educational programs, touching the lives of so many people. Thanks to you and your support, we have reached a work standard that has been recognized with accreditation by the American Alliance of Museums.

Your tax-deductible gift to the 2014 Annual Fund, large or small, truly makes a difference. [Last year, you helped with a generous gift of $XXX. Perhaps you will consider a small increase this year.] With a gift of $125, your name will be listed on our donor wall and in next year's honor roll.

Because of the generosity of good friends like you, the Michener will continue to teach, to engage, and to inspire.

So no need to worry if you can't find our earlier letter. Use this reminder to do the right thing for yourself and for this community.

On behalf of all of our visitors and the many people touched by the Michener, I thank you in advance for your generous support.

Sincerely,

Lisa Tremper Hanover
Director/CEO

Courtesy of the James A. Michener Art Museum

SAMPLE PHONE SCRIPT
OUR TOWN MUSEUM

(Use the ideas. Make the words your own.)

Hello, Mr./Mrs. _____, my name is _____ and I am a member of the board of Our Town Museum. How are you today?

Mr./Mrs. _____, I know that in the past you were a generous donor to the museum, and I'm calling tonight hoping you will renew that support. Last year, you gave $_____.

(PAUSE)

1. (IF YES, I'LL DO SOMETHING)
- Of course, we will be most grateful for whatever you give. But I want to tell you that gifts of $100 or more will be listed in our annual report. And to make it easy for you, I can take your charge information tonight.

(IF YES, I'LL GIVE A SPECIFIC AMOUNT)
- That's wonderful. Can we put that on a credit card? It will save us some mailing expenses so that your full gift goes toward our programs.
- (CONFIRM NAME, CREDIT CARD NUMBER, AND EXPIRATION DATE)

(IF $100 OR MORE, CONFIRM HOW NAME SHOULD BE LISTED)

2. (IF NO COMMITMENT/I'LL THINK ABOUT IT)
- Of course. Might I call you back in a few days? Your gift means so much to so many people.

3. (IF NO, I DON'T THINK SO/DEPENDING ON THE STRENGTH OF THE "NO")
- Of course, every gift helps. Can we count on you for $25? Whatever you could give would be a generous addition.

(BE PREPARED TO HEAR OBJECTIONS. SOME PEOPLE WILL USE THIS TIME TO VENT. DO NOT ARGUE. LISTEN, THANK THEM FOR THEIR RESPONSE, AND TELL THEM THAT YOU'LL SHARE THE FEEDBACK WITH OTHER BOARD MEMBERS.)

Mr./Mrs. _____, thanks so much for your time. We truly appreciate your support of the Museum of Our Town.

SAMPLE FORM 7.4

SAMPLE ANNUAL FUND PLEDGE CARD

YES! I want to make a special gift to the OUR TOWN MUSEUM

My tax-deductible gift is enclosed.

☐ $1,000   ☐ $500   ☐ $250   ☐ $100   ☐ $75   ☐ $50
☐ $25   ☐ $ _____

Name _____   Payment Method:

Address _____   ☐ Check enclosed ("Our Town Museum")

City/St_____   ☐ Charge my

Phone (day) _____   ☐ Visa ☐ Mastercard ☐ American Express

Email _____   Card#_____ Exp. _____

Signature _____

☐ My company will match this gift

Our Town Museum   Street Address   City, State Zip

Although the letter to the Board (sample form 7.6) was written for a capital campaign, the ideas could easily work for annual giving, too. The central idea is that board members discussed and approved the direction of the museum (strategic plan), the short-term goals for the museum, the budget for the museum (including the development plan), and in this case the plan for the new building as well as the plan to raise the necessary funds. After all that conversation, the board has responsibility—as a group and as individuals—for the success of the museum. As noted earlier, recruitment of new board members must include clarity of individual giving expectations. Discussions about a major campaign must include clarity of individual giving expectations. As a result of those discussions, a few people who are unwilling to give may choose to leave the board. One hundred percent of those who continue with the board must give.

SAMPLE TRIBUTE FORM

TRIBUTES

Yes, I wish to make a special gift of $_____ to the XYZ Museum.

I. This gift is from:

Name _____

Address _____

City _____ State _____ Zip _____

Phone _____ Email _____

2. Payment:

☐ Check enclosed (payable to "XYZ Museum")

☐ Charge

☐ Visa   ☐ Mastercard   ☐ American Express

Card # _____

Exp. Date _____

☐ My company will match this gift. Form enclosed.

3. This gift is made

☐ in honor of _____

☐ in memory of _____

4. Please notify:

Name _____

Address _____

City _____ State _____ Zip _____

Thank you for your thoughtfulness.

XYZ Museum is a 501 (c)(3) nonprofit organization, donations to which are tax-deductible to the fullest extent allowed by law.

XYZ MUSEUM   ADDRESS

SAMPLE BOARD LETTER

DATE

XXX
XXX
XXX

Dear XXX,

As best-selling author Luis J. Rodriquez has noted:

"Art is the heart's explosion on the world. Music. Dance. Poetry. Art on cars, on walls, on our skins. There is probably no more powerful force for change in this uncertain and crisis-ridden world than young people and their art."

Founded in 1974 by Latino artists and activists, Taller Puertorriqueño stands as testament to the wealth of possibilities created when citizens see a need in their community and decide to meet it. Taller Puertorriqueño is a force for change, **building community through art**. The Taller program includes:

- Cultural Awareness Program introduces young students to renowned local artists, performers, and educators who guide the children on a year-long journey of self-discovery.
- Youth Artists Program is a two-year program for talented high school sophomores, juniors, and seniors. With the guidance of professional artist mentors, students develop their artistic skills and produce a solid portfolio of work they can use to apply to arts colleges and universities.
- Visitenos is a program in which K–12 grade students engage in creative exploration of Latino cultures through videos of traditional dances, music records, and hands-on experiences with vejigante masks, drawing and painting, dance, and more.
- Memories in the Making is an innovative art therapy program that enables persons with dementia from the Hispanic/Latino community, for whom linguistic and cultural differences present additional barriers, to express themselves through art.
- The Eugenio Maria de Hostos Archives is a resource center that includes a varied collection of books, periodicals, articles, oral histories, and research—often out of print—focusing on Latino culture and history.
- The Lorenzo Homar Gallery is the region's only art gallery dedicated to Latin American and Caribbean art.
- Julia de Burgos Books and Crafts Store, a destination for original Latino artwork, crafts, handmade jewelry, and collectibles, serves as the only bilingual bookstore of its kind in the region. Augmenting the store is an ongoing series of book readings and author presentations.

- The annual <u>Arturo Schomburg Symposium</u> brings scholars from around the globe to Taller.

For more than three decades, Taller Puertorriqueño has been growing with the community, creating programs for all age groups, and reflecting the full range of Puerto Rican and Latin American cultural roots. Taller is now the largest and most established Latino arts and cultural organization in the Philadelphia region.

Now, in response to ever-increasing community demand, Taller is preparing to construct a new building so that more of our neighbors can be served. This new facility, to be designed by Puerto Rican architects Antonio Fiol-Silva and Modesto J. Bigas-Valedon (both with WRT in Philadelphia), provides numerous opportunities to remember and to honor.

<u>As a member of Taller's Board of Directors</u>, you know how hard we have worked and how far we have come. Through your efforts, we have become known as *el Corazón Cultural del Barrio*, the Cultural Heart of Latino Philadelphia.

Now I ask you to back up your work with your generosity. We, the leaders of Taller Puertorriqueño, must demonstrate our commitment to the new facility with full financial support. For grant requests, for corporate requests, and for community requests, we must have 100 percent board participation in our capital campaign. I know that we discussed a contribution amount for each member of the board. I hope that you will view that number as a minimum and, like our gold shovels will do soon, dig a little deeper.

I will be calling you soon about your gift. Please surprise me with your level of support.

Through art, we transform the Latino community's vision of itself. We remember the heritage that makes us who we are. Through your generosity, our new building will be a celebration of culture filled with pride.

Thank you so much.
Sincerely,

Edgardo González, Chair
Courtesy of Taller Puertorriqueño

Also note the emotional tug in this letter, the reference to cultural heroes, the pride of past successes, and the emphasis on community leadership. In reality, unlike most campaigns, individual giving was a relatively small part of this effort. The organization serves an extremely poor population. Much of the anticipated funding was from foundations and government sources, but for those efforts, a statement of 100 percent board participation was essential.

The full board did participate. The campaign went over its goal.

Many organizations send Christmas cards. I receive many, and I admit that I don't remember who sent what. I also know that in an increasingly diverse society, many people do not celebrate Christmas. But just about everyone in the United States celebrates Thanksgiving. So why not send a Thanksgiving card, get your message ahead of others, and actually be seen? Here is a sample with a very simple message:

THANKSGIVING 20XX

At this time of
Thanksgiving,
we are especially grateful
for all you have done
to make 20XX a very special year
for thousands of students in our community.

The Board and Staff of

Our Town Museum

Capital campaigns require an array of communications: solicitation materials, invitations, acknowledgment letters, signage, committee updates, etc. The list is long. Perhaps your museum has the funds to bring in consultants to write and/or design campaign literature. Or you may have this responsibility.

Because you will be working with a large number of people over a long period of time on a project that may not be fully planned, you must be mentally prepared for change. The beautifully worded description of the new wing may have to be tossed. The campaign chairman gets a job transfer out of state. The announced timeline for construction is suddenly extended. Who knows?

SAMPLE CIVIC PRIDE LETTER: CAPITAL

DATE

XXX
XXX
XXX

Dear XXX,

When you ride through our streets, you can feel what makes Delaware County so special.

Pride.

We live in a community that is proud of its homes, proud of its schools, and proud of its many cultural offerings. When people feel civic pride, they're likely to repair, to upgrade, and to invest.

Right now, many of our neighbors are investing in a source of hometown pride: the Community Arts Center. You may already know about the center's classes and workshops. More than 500 people, young and old, from dabbler to serious professional, come to the Center each quarter for art instruction. Others come to enjoy exhibitions, after-school programs, or the free summer concert series. Altogether, more than 14,000 people visit each year.

The Community Arts Center also goes to the community, bringing unique outreach programs to libraries, senior centers, and elementary and high schools. The center's good work is fundamental to the vitality of our region.

In its nearly sixty years, a lot of our neighbors have enjoyed the Community Arts Center, and so the building has become worn. The gallery space has been way too small, and the steps in the front have been a barrier. Fortunately, our Community Arts Center has a responsible group of stewards who are overseeing all the necessary improvements. A new, modern, 3,000-square-foot gallery is just about to open. Soon, windows and floors will be repaired. The main building will have a new, accessible entrance, an elevator to all floors, new classrooms, and a new gift shop.

We will have a new Arts Center to make us feel proud.

More than 90 percent of the necessary funds already have been raised from many good friends of the Community Arts Center. Numerous individuals and foundations have helped.

Now is the time to make an investment in our community's future. Pledges to the Community Arts Center Capital Campaign can be fulfilled in one, two, or three years. Gifts of $500 of more will receive special recognition. All campaign gifts are fully tax-deductible.

Whatever you choose to give, yours will be an important gift, a gift that underscores how valuable the Community Arts Center is to our life in Delaware County. Our goal is near at hand. Together, we're building a new Community Arts Center and a proud community. Thank you for joining us as we "go over the top."

Sincerely,

Courtesy of the Community Arts Center

SAMPLE CAPITAL PLEDGE FORM

OUR TOWN MUSEUM

CAMPAIGN FOR
EXCELLENCE PLEDGE FORM

Name(s) _____

Company (if applicable) _____

Address _____

City_____ **State** _____ **ZIP** _____

Phone _____ **Email** _____

I/We commit to Our Town Museum Campaign a total gift of $_____.

Your gift is <u>tax-deductible</u> to the extent of the law.

1. <u>Payment</u>

☐ Check Enclosed (payable to Our Town Museum)

☐ Charge $ _____ to my ☐ Visa ☐ MasterCard ☐ American Express

Name of Cardholder _____

Acct. # _____ Exp. Date _____ Sec. Code _____

Cardholder Signature _____

☐ This gift will be paid in part with a matching gift from _____

2. <u>Pledge</u> (payable over 3 years)

☐ I will fulfill this gift in the near future through a gift of stock.

☐ I will fulfill this pledge on the following schedule:

$_____ by June 30, 2015 $_____ by June 30, 2016 $_____
by April 30, 2017

Signature _____ **Date** _____

3. <u>Recognition</u>: Name as you wish to be listed _____

THANK YOU!

OUR TOWN MUSEUM   ADDRESS CITY, STATE ZIP

Here are a few campaign documents. Sometimes all the best advanced thinking doesn't quite work and the campaign stalls. I am sharing a letter that was created when it seemed that the campaign wouldn't quite hit the goal. Once again, the theme is pride. We gave particular emphasis on pride in place, both the building as place and the beautiful community as place.

Then you will find a sample of the expanded case statement and brochure copy that was used for a campaign that focused on the emotional connection community residents have to their place, historic Bucks County, Pennsylvania.

Notice how the need for this campaign, and all the others mentioned in this book, derives from community demand. The emphasis always is on people. Collections have no needs. Buildings do not have needs. People do.

SAMPLE FORM 7.9

SAMPLE PROSPECT WORKSHEET

JIM MARTIN   (wife=SARA)
200 West Elm Street
Littletown, PA 19901

610-232-0000 (h)

JIM is the former CEO of the Atlas Company. Atlas (manufacturers of paper widgets) was started by Jim's father in 1951, and Jim grew the company from $1 million annual sales to $210 million annual sales in 2012.

JIM retired in 2013, but continues to serve on the Atlas board.

JIM is a graduate of Michigan State University (BA in Psychology) and the Wharton School of Business (MBA).

He serves on the boards of Red Cross of Our Valley, United Way, the Eastside Shelter and the First Presbyterian Church of Littleton.

SARA MARTIN worked as a speech and language teacher prior to her marriage to JIM. For the past forty years, she has worked as a religious school teacher at the First

Presbyterian Church of Littleton. In addition, she serves on the boards of Welcome Wagon and the Valley Food Pantry.

JIM and SARA have two married children.

They own a vacation home in the Poconos.

They are avid collectors of first edition books, and they inherited from JIM's father (EZEKIAL) a collection of Civil War letters.

JIM and SARA MARTIN have been members at the $1,000 level since 2000.

Since 2004, they have made a special gift of $1,000 each year to the education department to fund a sign language interpreter for family programs.

In 1994, SARA was the co-chair of the Annual Gala.

THE ASK:

1. Thank them for their many years of generous memberships and additional contributions.
2. Share with them a letter you received from a young man who as a child benefitted from the sign language interpretation and has since gone on to a graduate program in museum management.
3. Discuss the Museum's plans to expand its family programs over the next two years.
4. Ask them if they would consider two important changes to their giving:
   a. To increase their membership support to $1,500 per year so that they can be members of the Leadership Circle.
   b. Increase their special gift each year so that interpreters can be hired for more programs.

Then be quiet. Let them respond.

Notes:

WAYS TO MAKE A GIFT TO OUR TOWN MUSEUM

I. GIFTS OF CASH

If you itemize on your tax return, cash gifts can be deducted, up to 50 percent of your adjusted gross income. On a $100,000 cash gift in a 35% percent bracket, you may save $35,000 in taxes. Our Town Museum invites cash pledges to the capital campaign payable over a period of years.

2. APPRECIATED STOCK

Appreciated stock (held more than one year) makes an excellent gift. You avoid all capital gain taxes (generally 15 percent of the appreciation) and will receive a charitable tax deduction for the stock's market value at the time of transfer.

3. BEQUEST THROUGH WILL OR TRUST

One of the simplest and most popular ways to make a gift that will live after you is to give through your will or trust. You can make a bequest to sustain Our Town Museum by providing a dollar amount, specific property, a percentage of your estate, or what is left (remainder) to Our Town Museum. Such a designation may reduce your estate taxes. In many cases a simple codicil to the will can add Our Town Museum and does not require rewriting your most recent will. Here is sample language:

I give, devise, and bequeath _____($) or _____(%) to Our Town Museum. Tax ID #XX-XXXXXXX. Our Town Museum may be reached at [address] or [phone].

4. RETIREMENT ACCOUNTS AND PENSION PLANS

Retirement account funds (IRAs or company plans) beyond the comfortable support of yourself or loved ones may be given to Our Town Museum by proper beneficiary designation. Large pension plan assets can be subject to double or triple taxation (federal income tax, state income tax, and federal estate taxes, if applicable). These taxes can substantially eliminate the benefit to heirs if tax-wise alternative planning is not arranged.

5. CDs, SAVINGS ACCOUNTS, BROKERAGE ACCOUNTS, CHECKING ACCOUNTS WITH P.O.D. PROVISIONS

P.O.D. stands for "Payable on Death." You retain full ownership and full control during your life. At your death, the account balance is paid to your named beneficiary, Our Town Museum, immediately and without probate.

6. CHARITABLE REMAINDER TRUSTS (ANNUITY AND UNI-TRUSTS)

Donors and spouses can benefit from lifelong payments from such a trust. The donor selects the rate of return from these income arrangements and also chooses a fixed or fluctuating annual payment to be made to the designated parties as long as they live. Estate and capital gain taxes may be completely bypassed and you will receive a current income tax deduction based on the age of the income recipient and the rate of return chosen.

7. GIFT OF LIFE INSURANCE

Insurance is another simple way to make a substantial future gift at a level that might not be possible with a cash gift. Name Our Town Museum as the owner and beneficiary to receive the proceeds of an existing life insurance policy. You will receive a tax deduction for approximately the cash surrender value, thereby reducing your tax liability in the year of the gift. An alternative is to simply add Our Town Museum as a revocable beneficiary. You retain the right to change this designation, but in this instance, you receive no income tax deduction.

☐ Gifts to Our Town Museum should be made with appropriate legal and/or financial counsel.

☐ Please let us know when you have made a planned gift by sending us a copy of the relevant section or paragraph of your legal document. By doing so, we will add your name to the membership of the Legacy Society.

SAMPLE CAPITAL CAMPAIGN CASE STATEMENT

We're proud.

All of us who live and work in Bucks County have the right to feel proud. Right in our midst, we have an outstanding art museum, and we built it just about by ourselves.

It was not that long ago that a handful of concerned citizens rallied in support of the idea of an art museum in Doylestown. The plan was to adapt the old Bucks County Prison into a place where children and adults would learn and celebrate the creative spirit. We may have had chutzpah. Certainly we had a vision.

That vision was to reclaim the artistic heritage of Bucks County. We knew that works of art that had been created in Bucks County were being acquired by private collectors and national museums. We were afraid that our children would never know how much our land, our farms, our river, and our canal had inspired others to create.

We were thinking about the future, and so, inspired by our beloved native son, the novelist James A. Michener, the community pulled together and did what it had to do, raising the funds to build a museum. The vision shared by so many individuals became a reality. Our museum has become a magnificent place, attracting visitors young and old, from near and far. The collections have grown. The standard of work has been so high that the James A. Michener Art Museum has been distinguished by accreditation from the American Association of Museums. We have reached an outstanding plateau.

Now, once again, we must think about the future. It is time to consider the ongoing changes in our community and in our museum. There are many more people living here now, more school children, more tourists, and more people from more varied backgrounds. No longer able to meet the demand of this larger and more diverse audience, the museum has outgrown its space.

The James A. Michener Art Museum has embarked on a $10 million capital campaign—the Michener Centennial Campaign honoring the one hundredth anniversary of the birth of our brilliant founder. In this effort, we are fortunate to have the talents and enthusiasm of two outstanding leaders: Ted Fernberger and Lou Della Penna. Many others will be involved as well, including our extraordinary director, Bruce Katsiff. A successful campaign will enable the museum to build upon its roles as a community-based institution and a renowned cultural destination.

Now is the time for concerned citizens to step forward and to do the right thing with as much generosity as possible. Now is the time to build upon the early vision for Bucks County.

Now is the time, once again, for everyone in Bucks County to give with pride.

Sincerely,

XXX

OUR HERITAGE

Artistic heritage defines Bucks County.

Since the time of itinerant artists in the eighteenth century, Bucks County has been home to thousands of artists whose influence extends far beyond any natural borders. Names like Garber and Redfield and Sheeler and Hicks are familiar both locally and nationally, as are Hammerstein, Perelman, Kaufman and Hart, and Parker and Buck.

These artists were drawn by the natural beauty of the area. The region's picturesque pastures, streams, quarries, farmhouses, and colonial villages provided a magnificent outdoor studio for creative work. Others were drawn—and continue to be attracted—by the convenience of travel to New York City and Philadelphia, by the chance to study with respected teachers, and by the tolerance that is rooted in the county's Quaker tradition.

Those qualities that attracted painters, sculptors, and writers to this region continue to be values deeply embedded in residents of Bucks County:

• Community-wide support for the arts
• A commitment to art education

Bucks County has been a quiet sanctuary for artists for more than 200 years—a place where some of our nation's best creative minds lived and worked as respected members of the community. By the mid-1960s, however, it was clear to James A. Michener that the artistic heritage—especially its paintings—that defined Bucks County was in danger of being lost. Works of art were disappearing from the area due to the lack of a local repository and by the transfer or sale of important paintings and drawings to private collectors and museums across America.

In 1988, a group of generous and civic-minded residents established the James A. Michener Art Museum to recapture the artistic heritage of Bucks County. In its first year, 100 objects formed the foundation of the collection, and the museum attracted 10,000 visitors.

The Michener is now home to the finest institutional collection of works by artists from the Bucks County region; most prominent among them are the painters who came to be known as the "Pennsylvania Impressionists," artists whose work was praised by the noted early twentieth-century painter and critic Guy Pène du Bois as "our first truly national expression." In only two decades, the collection has grown from 100 objects to more than 2,200.

Today, annual attendance at the Michener Art Museum exceeds 130,000 visitors who come for the museum's fifteen annual exhibits. The museum has become a venue for important traveling exhibits that engage visitors with the entire spectrum of art. Visitors enjoy classes, lectures, concerts, films, and other programs designed to develop a lifelong involvement with the arts. Educational activities serve more than 12,000 children annually. The Michener now has close to 12,000 members, a strong demonstration of the community's support and commitment.

The James A. Michener Art Museum has become one of the fastest growing and most important cultural centers in Southeastern Pennsylvania.

OUR CHALLENGE

Bucks County is growing. More than 600,000 people live here now. Some are college graduates, and some have little formal education. Some have deep roots in Pennsylvania, while others came here from across the country or around the world. Many are young families that have moved here to enjoy the quality of life. Some have never been to a museum, while others, passionate about art, are considering donations from their collections.

To meet the demands of this rapidly expanding and increasingly diverse community, the James A. Michener Art Museum must build upon the vision of our founders, preserving our artistic heritage and reaching out to multiple audiences with exemplary programs.

Four major challenges must be addressed today:

1. The museum has reached the limit of available gallery space. Many works in the collection must remain stored out of public view, and the current storage vault, built in 1993, is crammed with objects. There is no room for further significant acquisitions.
2. Space dedicated for special exhibitions is too small for many national touring exhibitions. The small square footage and low ceiling has forced the museum to turn down offers of numerous outstanding exhibitions and limited its ability to present large-scale work by today's artists.
3. Art preparation and handling areas are no longer up to the highest professional standards.
4. Education and public program spaces are inadequate to meet the increasing needs of the community. The small space available for programs has limited the number of classes, lectures, and concerts that can be offered. Likewise, facility rentals have been curtailed. Since many of these public space uses provide ticketing or fee opportunities, significant revenue enhancements have been lost.

OUR PLAN

To address these challenges, the Board of Trustees has selected the Hillier Group, one of the nation's leading architectural firms. The Hillier Group, known for creating environments that help shape human experience, will design a plan to address the Michener's current and future needs. The Hillier Group has completed projects in forty-one states and twenty-seven countries and has been honored with more than 250 national, state, and local design awards. Yet the firm's local roots in Princeton, New Jersey (where they have been located for forty years), ensure that they understand the importance of balancing regional pride with world-class achievements.

Securing the Future

The Michener has recently experienced significant growth in its endowment; a $6 million bequest from William D. Williams, an amateur painter himself and a frequent visitor to the Michener after retiring to Doylestown in 1990, ensures that the museum's endowment will support the operation of a larger facility.

In less than twenty years of existence, the Michener Art Museum has surprised even its most ardent supporters with phenomenal growth and the remarkable success of its programs, publications, exhibits, and collections. Through world-class exhibitions and innovative educational activities, the museum has truly become a force in the community, educating visitors about Bucks County artists while becoming a focal point of cultural activity in the region and engaging in beneficial partnerships with civic-minded individuals and organizations. In order to continue to grow and thrive, the Michener must successfully complete the Michener Centennial Campaign to fund these crucial capital improvements. Donors to the capital campaign can feel secure in knowing that their gifts to the Michener are sound investments in the collection, preservation, and interpretation of art in Bucks County, as well as sustaining the quality of life in the entire region.

A $3 million challenge grant from the Commonwealth of Pennsylvania and other early leadership gifts have provided a strong start for this campaign. With the help of individuals, foundations, and the business community, it will be possible to rise to the challenge issued by James A. Michener, who asked that people work "unstintingly" on the "big job at hand"—(to provide) *a world-class art museum that exhibits the best artists of Bucks County, and brings the best art to Bucks County.*

Join us in celebrating our heritage as we build for the future.

Phase I. A New Two-Level Wing ($6 million)

The first phase of the expansion and renovation program will create a new wing that will include a new 5,000-square-foot gallery on the upper level that will be large enough to accommodate major touring national exhibits. This exhibition space will also have the flexibility to be subdivided into smaller galleries for both traveling exhibits and the permanent collection.

This level will also house an orientation area where videos can be shown and visitors can be better prepared to enjoy the total museum experience. The new gallery design will create more effective circulation among the galleries than is currently available, allowing visitors to walk through the entire museum without retracing their steps.

The **lower level of the new wing** will improve and expand the museum's curatorial and administrative capabilities. Staff offices and a private study room will be created to meet the needs of professional staff and researchers. A state-of-the-art preparation and handling facility will also be established. Finally, new mechanical systems will be installed for the entire museum, which will include planned environmental innovations that will reduce long-term operating costs.

Phase II. Event Space Renovation and Expansion ($3 million)

To accommodate growing community and regional demand for access to the Michener while improving the museum's ability to sustain itself through earned income opportunities, the renovation will increase the functionality of the 4,000-square-foot sculpture garden and patio area. The patio area will be covered by glass to provide expanded space for public programs such as lectures, summer concerts, and other events. It will also be available for museum galas, jazz nights, demonstrations, and exhibition openings. This exciting, newly created indoor public space will greatly change the profile and functionality of the museum. It will become a premiere event resource for visitors from the growing communities of the region.

Phase III. Conversion of the Ann and Herman Silverman Pavilion into an Education Complex ($1 million)

Half of all Michener attendees, adults and children, visit the museum to participate in educational programs, which include art enrichment for pre-schoolers and elementary school students, art lessons and gallery tours for children, gallery talks, "meet the artist" programs, and concerts for adults.

Renovations to the Silverman Pavilion will allow the creation of two multipurpose classrooms and lecture spaces, an orientation area, and a children's gallery.

The proposed education complex will provide opportunities for diverse audiences to develop a lifelong appreciation for and involvement in the arts.

Courtesy of the James A. Michener Art Museum

CHAPTER EIGHT

FINAL THOUGHTS

No person was ever honored for what he received.
Honor has been the reward for what he gave.

—Calvin Coolidge

Refuge

S
ome months ago, I began a consulting assignment in a small city
(population about 150,000). I met with the organization's executive
director and board chairman for several hours. It was a good meeting in
which a number of key, perhaps controversial, issues were raised. That night,
I met a few friends for drinks and dinner at a local restaurant. To my great
surprise, among the many diners was the board chairman I had just met. She
came over to my table and began to chat about our earlier discussion. This
kind of encounter has happened to me often. Never mind that my friends
were sitting with me!

Earlier in *A Practical Guide to Fundraising for Small Museums: Maximizing the Marketing-Development Connection,* I made a distinction between
small museums in large cities and small museums in small towns. In a large
city, with hundreds of clubs and restaurants, it is less likely that you will encounter a donor during "off time." In a small town, this may happen often.
When I worked for smaller museums in small towns, I regularly met trustees
and donors in the supermarket, at the gym, at the movies, and, yes, at dinner. I found that I had to be "on" all the time I was "in town." In the oddest

places, I was asked about the next opening, about an upcoming special event, or about some detailed financial issue.

You need to find a place to relax and regroup. I had to travel to the next small city, thirty miles away, to occasionally remove myself from work-related encounters. Where will you go? The next town? The trail in the woods? Cards in your best friend's basement?

Plan now. You need down time.

Sometimes it is good to just talk about the weather.

Final Thoughts

Does anyone think small museum development is easy?

I have shared with you a long list of strategies and tactics. All of these will not be accomplished in a day, a month, or a year. Make your annual plan and stick to it. Next year, add something new.

Keep analyzing and evaluating. What worked and what didn't work? What actions stretched you to the brink? What language clicks? What new opportunities are coming up?

Hopefully, you have a colleague on staff with whom you can let off some steam. Use that relationship.

Some members of your staff may not understand what you do. They will see you planning parties, going to lunch, and meeting people for coffee, and they will wonder what all the fuss is about. Tell them. Plan with your CEO to put you on the agenda for a staff meeting and explain what you do. Share your development plan. Discuss your goals. Help them understand the relentless pressure you feel.

Some members of your community will not understand what you do. I have been asked whether mine is a full-time job. I want to answer, "No, it is *two* full-time jobs!"

Celebrate successes when they happen. The celebration may be as simple as a walk around the block or a box of donuts for your staff, but be sure to mark the key moments when they happen.

Take all the vacation time that is coming to you. Disconnect.

Plan in advance for the first day of the new fiscal year. I always find that day difficult as all the numbers go back to zero. Try to bask in the successes of the year that has closed.

Read novels. Your job is all about human relationships, the very stuff of good fiction.

Be curious. You are not on an island in your museum. Learn about your collections. Attend programs. Become articulate in the content of your organization.

Be kind to others.

Most important of all, be kind to yourself.

Final Thoughts: Selected Additional Resources

Crutchfield, Leslie R., and Heather McLeod Grant. *Forces for Good: The Six Practices of High-Impact Nonprofits.* San Francisco: Jossey-Bass, 2008.
Chronicle of Philanthropy
Guidestar.org (990 reports include list of board members, highest staff salaries)
National Council of Nonprofits
Network for Good
Boardsource
The Nonprofit Quarterly

Learn with your colleagues:
American Alliance of Museums
    Development and Membership Committee
    PR Committee
Small Museums Association
Regional Museum Associations: Southeastern Museums Conference, New England Museum Association, Mid-Atlantic Association of Museums, Western Museums Association, Association of Midwest Museums, Mountain-Plains Museums Association

DONOR BILL OF RIGHTS

*P*hilanthropy is based on voluntary action for the common good. It is a tradition of giving and sharing that is primary to the quality of life. To assure that philanthropy merits the respect and trust of the general public, and that donors and prospective donors can have full confidence in the not-for-profit organizations and causes they are asked to support, we declare that all donors have these rights:

To be informed of the organization's mission, of the way the organization intends to use donated resources, and of its capacity to use donations effectively for their intended purposes.

To be informed of the identity of those serving on the organization's governing board, and to expect the board to exercise prudent judgment in its stewardship responsibilities.

To have access to the organization's most recent financial statements.

To be assured their gifts will be used for the purposes for which they were given.

To receive appropriate acknowledgment and recognition.

To be assured that information about their donations is handled with respect and with confidentiality to the extent provided by law.

To expect that all relationships with individuals representing organizations of interest to the donor will be professional in nature.

To be informed whether those seeking donations are volunteers, employees of the organization or hired solicitors.

To have the opportunity for their names to be deleted from mailing lists that an organization may intend to share.

DONOR BILL OF RIGHTS

To feel free to ask questions when making a donation and to receive prompt, truthful and forthright answers.

The text of this statement in its entirety was developed by the American Association of Fund-Raising Counsel (AAFRC), the Association for Healthcare Philanthropy (AHP), the Council for Advancement and Support of Education (CASE), and the Association of Fundraising Professionals (AFP) and was adopted in November 1993.

INDEX

ABOUT THE AUTHOR

Sheldon Wolf is a marketing and development professional with nearly forty years of experience in nonprofit management in both the theater and museum industries. He has been a frequent presenter on marketing and development issues at conferences around the country for organizations including the American Association of Museums, the New England Museum Association, the Massachusetts Office of Travel and Tourism, the Pennsylvania Federation of Museums and Historic Institutions, the Massachusetts Board of Library Commissioners, Suffolk University, Drexel University, and the Southeast Museum Conference. For two years, he served as chairman of the 1,100-member Development and Membership Committee of the American Association of Museums (now the American Alliance of Museums). In addition, he has been a grant review panelist for the Heritage Philadelphia Program administered by the Independence Visitor Center Corporation and funded by the Pew Charitable Trusts, and for Project Stream, a program of the Pennsylvania Council on the Arts. After many years of advising colleagues on various management issues, Sheldon became an independent consultant in 2005 as president of Advancement Company, LLC. Since then, he has worked with more than forty organizations on a range of strategic planning, marketing, and development projects. Sheldon is also a playwright, and he has had productions of several plays in New York, New Jersey, and Pennsylvania. He earned a degree of Master in Fine Arts (Directing) from Brooklyn College and a degree of Bachelor of Arts (Theater/English) from Queens College. He is a member of Phi Beta Kappa.